# Let Freedom Ring!

BY Dale Evans Rogers

ANGEL UNAWARE
MY SPIRITUAL DIARY
TO MY SON
CHRISTMAS IS ALWAYS
NO TWO WAYS ABOUT IT!
DEAREST DEBBIE
TIME OUT, LADIES!
SALUTE TO SANDY
THE WOMAN AT THE WELL
DALE
COOL IT OR LOSE IT!
FINDING THE WAY
WHERE HE LEADS
LET FREEDOM RING!

# Let Freedom Ring!

## Dale Evans Rogers

with Frank S. Mead

FLEMING H. REVELL COMPANY
Old Tappan, New Jersey

*Library of Congress Cataloging in Publication Data*

Rogers, Dale Evans.
  Let freedom ring!

    1.  United States—Civilization.   2.   United States—
Religion.   3.   Patriotism—United States.   I.   Mead,
Frank Spencer, date   joint author.   II.   Title.
E169.1.R727       973        75-15922
ISBN 0-8007-0756-7

TO my beloved departed brother, Walter Hillman Smith—the second man in Hill County, Texas, to enlist in the United States Air Force during World War II. My brother served as a tower-control operator at Hickam Field, Hawaii, and on Okinawa. He believed in the American way of life and was ready to lay his life on the line to protect our wonderful heritage of freedom under God and the free-enterprise system.

TO our adopted son, John David (our Sandy), who asked our permission to join the Armed Forces at age seventeen because he wanted to be part of America's effort to fight oppression wherever she saw it and was asked to help. Our boy believed with all his heart in God and his country. Though partially handicapped, he was willing to serve however he was permitted.

TO all faithful Americans who have lived, fought, and died in order that freedom might ring and prevail in this country, and in others that desire it.

TO our founding fathers, who believed the Scripture: "Where the spirit of the Lord is, there is liberty" (2 Corinthians 3:17); and fearlessly carved out our magnificent charter with no thought of the cost to themselves, their families, and their fortunes.

God grant that their labor of love and sacrifice will not be in vain!

# Contents

# "Read It and Pray!"

I want to be a part of the answer—
I want to keep Old Glory flying high—
I want to keep aflame the torch of freedom—
I want to pass it on when I die.
For there is so much good in this country—
But all you hear about is the wrong—
I want to hear a cheer for the Nation—
I want so sing her Star-spangled song.
   I love the thirteen stripes of the red and white
   That represent a courageous fight,
   To put the fifty stars on the patch of blue,
   Fifty states for me and you!
And for the troubles we have, there's a solution—
For God has given a Book to show the way—
They read the Bible and wrote the Constitution
We'd better start to read and pray!

DALE EVANS ROGERS
(written and sung in our
inspirational "God and Country"
spot in personal appearances)

# Introduction

It seems like only yesterday that I went down to Ocean
Grove, New Jersey, to witness to the International
Bible Class Convention, and sat at dinner with my good
friend, the esteemed editor of the Fleming H. Revell
Company, Dr. Frank S. Mead, to talk about our "next"
book. We discussed several ideas, but none of them
"sparked." We wandered off into a discussion of the
Bicentennial celebration coming up in 1976—and out of
the blue, the spark hit the powder keg. Why not a book
about America—America and God—you know! Something like "Let Freedom Ring"—and we were off and
running.

Dr. Mead said, "Look, Dale, this country is going
through some pretty rough times right now. We've had
Vietnam and Watergate and corruption and scandals all
over the place, and inflation, and decreases in church
membership and loss of interest in the church. A lot of
people have just about thrown in the sponge and lost
hope in a system and a way of life that began with the

ringing of the Liberty Bell. We are being told that no democracy has ever lasted more than two hundred years, so we'd better get set for the funeral. But there are a lot more who don't buy that at all—who still respect and love the heritage of the American past and have confidence in the American future. Let's give them a lift—a book that will tell us what is *good* about America, and how to make it even better. Why don't you wave the flag, and sound that bugle, in a rootin' tootin', unashamed declaration of what you feel about our country?"

That is *exactly* what I intend to do. It's been bubbling in my mind for some time. I'm fed up with the arm-chair critics and the wild-eyed non-Americans who do nothing but sneer and complain. That kind of thinking didn't build this country or do anything to preserve or protect it. This country was conceived and built by people who were not afraid to put their shoulders to the wheel and their lives on the line for their nation's future.

Call me a flag-waver, if you will. I love that flag—and all it stands for. I'm a square: that old song, sung and written by George M. Cohan, "You're a Grand Old Flag" still hits me in the heart.

Call me reactionary, if you will. That doesn't bother me, one bit. Yes, I am reacting strongly, and I'm ready to be stronger. I am calling on those of you who love your God and your country to act wherever you are— whenever you can—with faith in Almighty God to make this nation one under Him. With no apology whatever, I am blatantly patriotic, even naïvely so. Call me by any of the names and adjectives now in vogue among these people who enjoy getting the "in" feeling by degrading their country, but keep this straight and clear: I am about to raise this flag of the United States of America in grateful love and praise.

The Bible says, "Blessed is the nation whose God is the Lord" (Psalms 33:12). America was founded on faith in just such a God, on His Word (the Holy Bible), on faith and trust in each other, on a conviction that all men and members of a brotherhood in which all are free and equal. We have survived some terrible troubles in the past two hundred years. I believe that just as God saved His people in Israel and brought them through their disasters—when they turned to Him in repentance —even so has He done and will do it for us in our little American section of His vineyard. Jesus said, "Other sheep I have which are not of this fold: them also must I bring . . ." (John 10:16). We are a part of His flock in America.

When I went to Jerusalem in 1972, a rush of emotion almost overwhelmed me as I entered the gates of that holy city. A feeling of coming home engulfed me. When I left it, some days later, I felt that I was leaving my true home. Jerusalem, O Jerusalem! I heard Him calling to me as I entered, "Come home! Come home!" But I was to discover that He calls to me in Hollywood, in America, too. Come home, America! "Come now, and let us reason together . . . though your sins be as scarlet, they shall be as white as snow" (Isaiah 1:18). It is not too late for our tottering society to be restored, strengthened, and turned from our destruction-bound paths—not too late to answer the challenge and glory of an upward climb with God into a new and better future.

I love my flag. I love my country. I love my God. I have great faith in all three.

Of course we have made mistakes. Of course, we have faults. Who—and what—doesn't? Do you know of *any perfect* system or organization? Do you know of any church, school, business, family—any human life in which no mistakes are made? But I am convinced that the minority, which would tear down this democracy, is indeed a *minority,* and that those Americans who go quietly about living their American way and fulfilling the American Dream are the vast majority.

Let me illustrate that. Mr. Charles L. Gould, the publisher of the *San Francisco Examiner,* gave an address in which he stressed "The Positive Side." Here is what he said:

> Many times, as we pick up the daily papers, or listen to the news on radio or TV, the world around us appears extremely bleak. Let's stop for a minute, however, and look at the other —the positive—side. The vast majority of our people—regardless of race, creed, color, or economic status—are respectable, reasonable, responsible citizens.
>
> Last year, for example:
> More than 196,000,000 of our people were not arrested.

More than 89,000,000 married persons did not file for divorce.
More than 115,000,000 individuals maintained a normal affiliation with some religious group.
More than 75,000,000 citizens, and corporations, paid more than $160 billion in income taxes.
More than 49,000,000 students did not riot or petition to destroy our system.
More than 9,000,000 of our young men did not burn their draft cards.
More than 4,000,000 teachers, preachers, and professors did not strike or participate in riotous demonstrations.
I have no apologies to make for my country or my generation. Never before in history has a people accomplished so much, given so much, or asked for so little.

Don't let anyone sell you the idea that ours is a sick society. It is far from perfect, but it is also far and away the most enlightened, most unselfish, most compassionate in the world's history.

Let those apostles of despair who preach hate and disorder ask themselves what they have done and what they are doing for the good of their loved ones, their nation, and the world.

*Sunshine Magazine,* January 1972

Hook, bait, and sinker, I buy that. With Mr. Gould, I know that this America and these United States are not perfect beyond improvement—any more than any man or woman who walks this earth is perfect beyond improvement. But when we confess all our mistakes, it is still interesting to me that while there are millions of people in other countries who would like to *come* here, there are precious few who want to *leave* it.

It all reminds me of the student in one of our colleges who wrote on a campus wall, AMERICA IS UGLY. Someone came along later and added something to this: CUT YOUR HAIR SO YOU CAN SEE IT BETTER.

Now let's see what is better about it that commands our allegiance. Let's start with the days when something better was planted in our soil . . . .

DALE EVANS ROGERS

# Let Freedom Ring!

# 1

# Concept

My country, and my God! With all that is within me, I love both, and I put my faith in both—for to me they are as closely connected as cause and effect, heart and mind, body and soul. This America was no historical or geographical accident; it was an idea in the mind of God before it became earthly reality and one of His noblest creations. It didn't just happen; it was—and is—a part of His purpose for mankind.

Slowly, oh, how slowly, did it come into being! James Michener, in his book *Centennial,* calculates that there were "one billion, seven hundred million years of activity" before this land was ready for any habitation. God was in no hurry; this must be a *good* land, laid on "how firm a foundation."

At first, Michener explains, it was no more than turbulent chaos; the earth writhed and groaned in its pains of birth. Mountains skipped like rams and little hills like lambs; they rose and fell back through the crust of the earth, and new hills and mountains appeared and reached for the sky, elsewhere. Volcanoes created hills and valleys, great peaks and plains, land that was to be fertile and land that would be desert. Great glaciers crawled like colossal landmovers, changing the contours of the land, melting at last to create rivers that flowed in torrent from mountain to plain, leaving gold in the river beds, hiding silver, iron, copper, lead—a wealth beyond price—in soil and rock. In His time came trees, grass, flowers, mastodons and dinosaurs. Then the climate changed and these monsters died; they were never intended to dominate the land, but in their day they were wild and free. *That* was planted in our very soil and souls.

When the first Indian appeared, he too lived wild and free; of superior intellect, he hunted down the bisons that roved by the millions and shot down eagles and put their feathers on his head. Twenty-five thousand years ago there were Indians here, and for centuries they roamed a land that stretched from sea to sea—roamed it in widely separated bands and tribes, and it was their land, wherever their tepees stood. Free as the winds were the Indians, free as the rivers that flowed to the seas. Yet it was never in the destiny of 400,000 red men to have and hold dominion over a land promised to greatness and power in the world. Its vastness was too much for one race.

Yet the Indian did represent a long step forward in the divine purpose; he was a vast improvement upon the beast, for he sensed the presence of invisible gods and spirits all about him—gods speaking to him in the wind, in rain and the sun and moon and trees, from whose hands came life and death, disease and delight, good harvest and draught, in thunder and flowing water, and the Indian danced and feasted for and to them. Above all these lesser gods was a Great Spirit to which they prayed, but in fear and not in love and understanding. The Chippewas had a Voyagers' Prayer:

> O Great Spirit!
> Thou hast made this lake;
> Thou hast also created us Thy children;
> Thou art able to make this water calm
> Until we have safely passed over.

But even their Great Spirit could not save them from the relentless attack of a new brand of man who came against them. This man's face was not red but white. The

Indian fought him with primitive tomahawk, bow and arrow, and stone-tipped spear—a Stone Age people struggling for survival. The white man brought weapons of iron and gunpowder, axes that leveled their forests, ploughs that cut deep into the earth—and Bibles. The scattered, wandering tribes fought desperately to stem the tide but they could not possibly win. They were forced out, in the words of Jesse Hays Baird "by cosmic forces beyond the control of any man or nation." The manner in which the white man all but annihilated them is a fearful chapter in our history books which we would like to forget.

Came the bitter winter day in 1620 when a handful (102) of refugees from the bigotry and injustice, the greed, and prejudices of Old World Europe came ashore in Cape Cod Bay with the dream of a more godlike government burning in their hearts. Before they put foot on the soil of the new land, they huddled in the cabin of the tiny *Mayflower* and forty-one of them signed a Compact which began with the words, *In the Name of God, Amen.* They looked upon this frozen, hostile land as the place in which they would, as General Washington put it a century later, conduct "an experiment intrusted to the hands of the American people." All life is an experiment, but an experiment under God takes high priority over all the rest. So, with their commonwealth dedicated to God, the survivors of that relentlessly hard voyage knelt in the snow to thank Him for safe passage, and the American Dream began.

# 2

# The Founders

The Pilgrims were not the first nor the last Europeans to
set foot on these shores; Norsemen were here before
they were, and so were the Spaniards (there is also a claim
that the Irish were here, too!), but they were the first to
come seeking a freedom that was as spiritual as it was

political or economic. Dr. Robert J. McCracken reminds us that "We on this continent should never forget that [these] men crossed the Atlantic not to find soil for their ploughs but to secure liberty for their souls." True, they were sponsored by a British commercial company, but for them—from beginning to end—it was a pilgrimage for God and conscience. All they wanted was to be good on God's formula, and to help others to be good, and to live as free men under a new form of government in which God alone was King. It is significant that once they had built log cabins to live in, they built a log meeting-house (church) which was also a fortress, complete with pulpit and gunports.

There were 102 of them on the *Mayflower;* before their first terrible winter was over, nearly half of them were dead and buried in the village street (so the Indians would not know how many of them were gone). Thirteen of the eighteen wives perished. The survivors walked over their graves to plant corn in the first warm days of Spring. But when the *Mayflower* sailed back to England, there was not a single Pilgrim—man, woman, or child— aboard.

To that *spirit,* that *faith,* that *courage,* I pledge allegiance with all that is within me.

First the trickle, then the niagara of immigrants: more English (Puritans—the English Puritans differed from the Pilgrims of Plymouth Colony. The Pilgrims were Separatists; that is, they left the Church of England. The Puritans remained in the Church in an effort to "purify" it.) Then there were the Dutch, French, Scots, Swedes;

and those of varying faith and doctrine—Baptists, Quakers, Presbyterians, Roman Catholics, Wesleyans, Calvinists, Moravians, Covenanters, Lutherans. Few if any of them were what you might call wealthy; most of them were poor. All of them were "of a dream possessed." Perry Miller says of the Bay Company (the Puritans) that they were not "a battered remnant of suffering Separatists thrown upon a rocky shore; it was an organized task force of Christians, executing a flank attack on the corruption of Christendom."

Let freedom ring!

Emma Lazarus may have had them in mind when she called our Statue of Liberty "Mother of Exiles," and had her say:

> Keep, ancient lands, your storied pomp!
> .    .    .    .    .    .    .    .
> Give me your tired, your poor,
> Your huddled masses yearning to breathe free,
> The wretched refuse of your teeming shore,
> Send these, the homeless, tempest-tost to me,
> I lift my lamp beside the golden door.

These early ones were primarily English, and they loved Mother England. But now three thousand miles of saltwater separated them. This land, this Dream, separated them—cut them off—from the Old World. Gradually —inevitably—the apron strings which bound them to Mother England strained and snapped. Differences and debates accumulated; one ideology supplanted the other; new loyalties superseded the old. England was stubborn and determined to hold them, sending troops to put down a rising rebellion. A riot flared in Boston; that night there was a meeting of the rebels in Faneuil Hall; they sent a message to the British lieutenant requesting that he "issue his orders for the immediate removal of the troops." Instead, more troops were sent to hold down the lid.

One night in April, 1775, a British column marched on Lexington and Concord to take an arsenal, and Paul Revere leaped to the saddle. It was the beginning: eight Americans died at Lexington, ten more at Concord. The debates were over. This was war.

A handful of men—farmers, clerks, workmen, ordinary men possessed of extraordinary courage—faced the troops of the mightiest military power on earth that day. Loathe war as we will, there is something about it that stirs respect and admiration in the heart of the patriot. They fought for their land, for their cause, for the future. Eighteen Americans died that day, and more of the British. Today, near the Concord Bridge, you see the grave of some of the British dead—buried under a tombstone containing this inscription:

THEY CAME THREE THOUSAND MILES, AND DIED
TO KEEP THE PAST UPON ITS THRONE.

Too late!

Now Richard Henry Lee of Virginia introduced a resolution in the Continental Congress at Philadelphia, declaring "That these United Colonies are, and of Right ought to be Free and Independent States, that they are absolved from all Allegiance to the British Crown, and that all political connection between them and the state of Great Britain is, and ought to be totally dissolved. . . ." And a tall, gangling red-headed young man named Thomas Jefferson took that resolution and put it into a Declaration of Independence which was the birth certificate of the new nation. It is a Declaration shot through with the ethical and moral concepts of Christianity.

Fifty-six men signed it, pledging their allegiance:

> And for the support of this Declaration, with a firm Reliance on the Protection of the divine Providence, we mutually pledge to each other our Lives, our Fortunes and our sacred Honor.

The Declaration is as much spiritual as it is political. Like our Constitution, it has its source and its roots in religious conviction.

Ben Franklin warned them, before they signed, that they must all hang together or they would all hang separately. None of them hanged, but some of them paid a fearful price for it. Here is what happened:

Five signers were captured by the British as traitors, and tortured before they died. Two lost their sons in the Continental Army; Abraham Clark had two sons captured. Carter Braxton of Virginia, and Lewis Morris, a wealthy planter and trader, saw their ships swept from the seas by the British Navy. Braxton sold off his property to pay his debts and died in poverty. Robert Morris also lost his shipping business. Thomas McKean was so hounded by the British that he was forced to move his family constantly; his possessions were taken from him, and he died bankrupt. The list of those who lost homes, properties and fortunes is a long one; it includes signers Ellery, Clymer, Hall, Walton, James Smith, Hewes, Hooper, Gwinnett, Heyward, Rutledge, Middleton, Lewis, Morris, Floyd, Stockton, Hopkinson, Taylor.

At the battle of Yorktown, Thomas Nelson, Jr., noticed that General Cornwallis had taken over the Nelson home for his headquarters; he urged General Washington to open fire and watched his house go up in flames. Francis Lewis had his home and property destroyed; the enemy jailed his wife, and thanks to brutal treatment, she died in jail. John Hart was driven from his wife's bedside as she lay dying; for more than a year he lived in forests and caves, returned home to find his wife dead and his thirteen children vanished. A few weeks later he died of exhaustion and a broken heart. Lewis Morris and Livingston suffered similar fates.

These were not wild-eyed, rabble-rousing ruffians. They were soft-spoken men, of distinction and education. Standing straight and tall and unwavering, they pledged "our Lives, our Fortunes, and our Sacred Honor."

The war lasted just eight years to the day. Then the soldiers went home without a farthing in their pockets. They had a nation but it, too, was bankrupt. It also had near-anarchy, chaos, and confusion. For four years more they struggled to form a perfect union of the States, or colonies; debates became hotter and hotter, mobs formed in the streets; and after many weeks of this, the men selected to write a constitution were about ready to give up and go home. They might have done just that, had not old Ben Franklin taken the floor and spoken to them:

> I have lived a long time, sirs, a long time; and the longer I live the more convincing proofs I see of this truth: "that God governs in the affairs of men." . . . We have been assured, sirs, in the sacred writings, that "Excepte the Lord build the house, they labor in vain that build it." I firmly believe this. And I also believe that without his concurring aid, we shall succeed in this political building no better than the building of Babel. We shall be divided . . . our projects will be confounded and we, ourselves, shall become a reproach and byword to future ages . . . . I therefore beg leave to move: That hereafter prayers, imploring the assistance of Heaven and its blessings on our deliberations, be held in this assembly every morning before we proceed to business . . . .

That did it. From that moment on, they made progress. They put the principles laid down in the Declaration into law—creating the Constitution and a Bill of Rights that have become the envy and the model of free men and nations all across the world—and as clear as the Ten Commandments. Wendell Phillips said of it, "All that is valuable in the Constitution is one thousand years old"—as old, that is, as the One who said, ". . . Know the truth, and the truth shall make you free" (John 8:32).

Coming one day out of the Constitutional Convention, Ben Franklin was stopped by a suspicious old lady who asked him, "Sir, what kind of government have you given us?" Ben replied, "A Republic, madam, if you can keep it."

Well, on the whole, we haven't done too bad a job, in the past, of keeping it, and of preserving, protecting, and defending the Constitution of the United States. But the past is prologue. What about it in the here and now? Can we keep it, hold fast with it against all the new, furious storms that are pounding at its base?

I believe we will. I believe we have to—if we are to survive. You know, there is an old crumbling rock out here in our West, known as Spirit Rock. It got its name from the Indians, who worshiped at its base and offered there the sacrifices that they thought would appease the Great Spirit. But it is crumbling now, and I suppose, some day, there won't be very much left of it. I think of our Constitution as *our* Spirit Rock, to which and for which generations of men have made the last supreme sacrifice of their lives. But if the precious principles of freedom, brotherhood and justice ever crumble *within* our hearts, it will be the end not only of the Constitution, but of *us*.

Let freedom ring! Let it begin with *me!*

# 3

# I Am The United States

So they had their United States. It's odd that one who is not respected by many in this country today gave the country its new name. It was Tom Paine (who had written on a drumhead at Valley Forge that "these are the times that try men's souls . . .") who first called this country "The United States of America."

Now what would they do with it?

What they did with it—and what successive genera-
tions have made of it—is brilliantly described by Otto
Whittaker, in this little piece, which he called "I Am the
Nation."

I was born July 4, 1776, and the Declaration
of Independence is my birth certificate. The
bloodlines of the world run in my veins because I offered freedom to the oppressed. I
am many things, and many people.

**I AM THE NATION.** I am 20,000,000 living
souls—and the ghosts of millions who have
lived and died for me. I am Nathan Hale and
Paul Revere. I stood at Lexington and fired the
shot heard around the world. I am Washington, Jefferson, and Patrick Henry. I am John
Paul Jones and the Green Mountain Boys, and
Davy Crockett. I am Lee and Grant and Abe
Lincoln.

**I REMEMBER THE ALAMO,** the *Maine,*
and Pearl Harbor. When freedom called, I
answered and stayed until it was over, over
there. I left my heroic dead in Flanders Fields,
on the rock of Corregidor, and on the bleak
slopes of Korea. I am the Brooklyn Bridge, the

wheatlands of Kansas, and the granite hills of Vermont . . . I am big; I sprawl from the Atlantic to the Pacific. I am more than 4,000,000 farms. I am forest, field, mountain, and desert. I am quiet villages and cities that never sleep.

**YOU CAN LOOK AT ME** and see Ben Franklin walking down the streets of Philadelphia with his breadloaf under his arm. I am Babe Ruth and the World Series. I am 169,000 schools and colleges and 250,000 churches, where my people worship God as they think best. I am a ballot dropped in a box, the roar of a crowd in a stadium, and the voice of a choir in a cathedral. I am an editorial in a newspaper and a letter to a Congressman. I am Eli Whitney and Stephen Foster. I am Tom Edison, Albert Einstein, and Billy Graham. I am Horace Greeley, Will Rogers, and the Wright Brothers. I am George Washington Carver, Daniel Webster, and Jonas Salk. I am Longfellow, Harriet Beecher Stowe, Walt Whitman, Thomas Paine.

**YES, I AM THE NATION.** I was conceived in freedom and, God willing, in freedom will I spend the rest of my days. May I always possess the integrity, the courage, and the strength to

keep myself unshackled, to remain a citadel of
freedom and a beacon of hope to the world.

That is magnificent. It describes the spirit of
America—or the unfolding of the spirit which has made
us what we are, from Paul Revere in 1775 to Jonas Salk
and Billy Graham in 1975. I believe in every word of it.

But if Mr. Whittaker will forgive me, I'd like to add
something to all this. I think America is all he says it
is—and something more, vastly more.

When the United States entered World War II, an
article appeared in one of our magazines explaining why
we entered it. Among other reasons, the author said,
American boys were fighting for the privilege of going
down to the corner drugstore to buy an ice-cream soda,
the right to play ball, or work in a factory, or an office,
or on a farm, to go to church or college, or go fishing as
they pleased and when they pleased. That left me a
little cold; I thought we were fighting for something a
lot more important than *that!* For, to me, America is not
a spot of earth on which we can "do our thing" (whether
it is significant or insignificant), but a land in which we
make some contribution to the rights and welfare of
others, and to the common good of American democracy. It's been said, "Most of all, America is a state of
mind—a point of view—a love of moving on—beyond
the next hill—the next filling station—the next frontier
—expanding—growing—living beyond the horizon.
That's America. That's the USA!"

"When an American says he loves his country," said

Adlai Stevenson, "he means not only that he loves the New England hills, the prairies glistening in the sun, the wide and rising plains, the great mountains and the sea. He means that he loves an inner air, an inner light in which freedom lives and in which a man can draw the breath of self-respect."

Now let's take a look at that inner air and light.

# 4

# The Source and Ground
# of Freedom

We Americans are a proud people—proud of our heritage, our way of life, our prosperity, our mountains and our hills, and our reputation for being a kindly big brother to the world. Above all, we are aggressively proud of something we call *freedom*. That word has top priority in our American dictionary. We boast of being a free people, with freedom of speech and press, free ballots, free enterprise, free churches, free public schools, free in opportunity to become anything from a stripper to a saint. The land of the free and the home of the brave! We sing it out for all the world to hear:

> Our fathers' God, to Thee,
> Author of liberty,
> To Thee we sing.

We love it so much that we'd like to see every country in the world have it and enjoy it, as we do.

*Freedom!* It's a word that is in our blood and on our tongues—but ask any ten Americans just what this freedom *is,* and why he should pledge his allegiance to it, and you'll be surprised at the answers you'll get. It is a beautiful word—and a dangerous one. It can be a blessing or a two-edged sword. If you don't believe that, go down to the Arlington National Cemetery in Virginia and take a look at what it has cost us to get it.

Educator Ernest O. Melby says that "No generation of Americans has talked so much about freedom as the present generation and none has shown so great a readiness to abandon it." Correct. We kick this word around like a football, or like football players who have forgotten where the goal posts are. We play with it for all sorts of purposes, good and bad. Let's start now, to sort it all out and find out just what *American* freedom is, and what it *isn't.*

**Freedom is not** a political football.

**Freedom is not** something handed down from generation to generation, like the family silver or the old cuckoo clock; it is something that has to be won by every succeeding generation.

**Freedom is not** a trophy cup won for us by our dead ancestors; it is a continuing process of which we are a vital part.

**Freedom is not** the right to get anything we want, no matter how. ("Your freedom ends where my nose begins.")

**Freedom is** more of a headache than an heirloom—always a responsibility and never a license. When a youngster was asked to describe the famous picture, *The Spirit of '76,* he said, "Well, in it there's one man with a fife and another with a drum, and another with a headache."

**Freedom is,** above all, not an economic or nationalistic paradise. *It is a religious discovery.*

When Thomas Jefferson sat down at his portable, handmade desk in a dingy lodging house in Philadelphia to write the Declaration of Independence, he had a great idea in the back of his mind. He may have asked himself, "Can the liberties of a nation be thought secure, when we have removed their only firm basis, a conviction in the minds *of the people* that these liberties are the gift of God? That they are not to be violated but by His wrath? I tremble for my country when I reflect that God is just; that His justice cannot sleep forever."

The words "of the people" are important; already, Jefferson knew, the people had a (Biblical) conviction that ". . . where the Spirit of the Lord is, there is liberty" (2 Corinthians 3:17). Look at them: Puritans in Massachusetts, Anglicans in the South, Irish and Scots and Germans and British Quakers in Pennsylvania—*all* of them thought of liberty and freedom as something divinely inspired.

Jefferson was aware of the fact that politics and economics were twin roots of the war to come, but he also knew that until you strike the shackles of the soul from men, you can never strike the shackles of human tyranny from his wrists. So he wrote this immortal line, at the very beginning of the Declaration:

> We hold these Truths to be self-evident, that all Men are *created* equal, that they are endowed by their Creator with certain unalienable Rights, that among these are Life, Liberty, and the Pursuit of Happiness (italics mine).

That had nothing to do with politics or the economy; that was intensely *religious*. It was, as someone has said, "the most seminal sentence in the history of American values."

Just as the author of Genesis says in the first verse of the Bible, "In the beginning God created the heaven and the earth," Jefferson wrote that from the beginning of the American nation the Creator had his hand in it and upon it.

Of course there had been men who fought for freedom long before Thomas Jefferson was born—as far back as Moses and Socrates. But, says David H. C. Read, famous pastor of the Madison Avenue Presbyterian Church, in a great sermon, "What Moses knew, what Socrates in his own way perceived, and what the greatest of our Founding Fathers understood was that real human liberty is not something to be realized in abstraction from the disciplines of the mind and spirit that seek to know the truth about human life. Liberty and independence are empty words unless we have some conception of *what human beings are meant to be,* unless there is some inner vision of a life *designed by some greater power than ours.*"

Yes, truth-seekers have always been with us. And they have always popped up with Pilate's old question, "What is truth?" (John 18:38). Jesus arrived on our earth with a new truth about truth: He said, "I am the way, the truth, and the life . . ." (John 14:6). *I, Christ, the Son of God.* Up until the moment He said that, the old Ten Commandments, the Jewish Law, had been the infallible guide to all who sought God's truth and way, but now they had One who came to fulfill that Law, to give it wider, deeper dimensions. He meant us to try, the very best we can, to keep the Law—and, when we fail—to find new strength in His mercy and grace (sufficient to pardon and strengthen us) *to go on trying.*

This America of ours is a holy experiment, and not yet

an accomplished fact. This America—God knows and we know—is far from perfect, but at least we are *trying*. We had sown in our hearts the seed of freedom: its growth now depends upon *us,* and not on any president or statesman or soldier.

We've come a long way, but we still have a long way to go if we are to measure up to *God's* definition of freedom. If we can follow Christ's advice to ". . . seek ye first the kingdom of God, and his righteousness . . ." (Matthew 6:33), we can indeed be free. If we fail, what freedom we have can and probably will die on the vine.

# 5

# Freedom of Speech

Before we got ourselves mixed up in World War II, President Roosevelt said something about freedom which will ring liberty bells in our minds long after we've forgotten who said it. It was this:

> In the future days, which we seek to make secure, we look forward to a world founded upon four essential human freedoms.

The first is freedom of speech and expression—everywhere in the world.

The second is freedom of every person to worship God in his own way—everywhere in the world.

The third is freedom from want—which, translated into world terms, means economic understandings, which will secure to every nation a healthy peacetime for its inhabitants —everywhere in the world.

The fourth is freedom from fear, which translated into world terms, means a worldwide reduction in armaments to such a point and in such a thorough fashion that no nation will be in a position to commit an act of physical aggression against any neighbor—anywhere in the world.

I know! Some of you will say, "Humph!" when I mention Franklin D. Roosevelt. (I'm told that some ardent Roosevelt-haters won't even carry a dime in their pockets, because the dime has his picture on it!) But let's stop being partisan for a moment, and let his statement stand on its own legs. Let's look for whatever truth there may be in it. There's a lot of truth in it, and a lot of inspiration in it, no matter who said it.

The president, you will notice, was thinking of freedom in *world terms;* after each point, he said, *"Everywhere in the world."* Let's break that down into "everywhere in

The United States" (for Freedom—like charity—begins at home). If we want to help all the world live free, we have to be free first. We can't give anything we haven't got.

He put *freedom of speech and expression* first among the four, and that's more than interesting.

Some of us think that freedom of speech (and freedom of the press) came to us in the First Amendment to the Constitution. Wrong. It was guaranteed in the First Amendment, but the process of getting it began long before that—even before the Declaration of Independence and the War of the Revolution. The fight for it began when the Pilgrims and the Puritans left England for our shores—and the battle for it still goes on.

Back in 1710 sixty-five years before Concord and Lexington—a young German named John Peter Zenger arrived in New York with some good ideas and a lot of courage and a stubborn habit of speaking his mind. He played the organ in church and his wife taught Sunday school. By 1733 he was publishing the *New York Weekly Journal;* in 1734 he was arrested for printing and publishing "several Seditious Libels . . . many Things tending to raise Factions and Tumults . . . among People of this Province, inflaming their Minds with contempt of His Majesty's Government and Greatly disturbing the Peace thereof . . . ." The point was that John Peter didn't think much of His Majesty's Governor of New York—William Cosby, a haughty, pompous, and corrupt dictator. Zenger said things that made the governor furious; he wrote a series of doggerel songs that were read in the taverns and sung in the streets. (Four of them were burned by the public hangman.) He ridiculed and satirized His Majesty's Governor. Cosby called him an enemy and traitor, and had him arrested and brought to trial. The charge: libel.

What followed was one of the most important trials in American history. Actually, Zenger was on trial for daring to speak the truth about a bad governor and government. The real issue, however, was freedom of speech. Zenger was acquitted, and there was more singing and dancing in the streets. A climate of opinion had begun to form in America that led eventually to the Revolution. Gouverneur Morris called it "the morning star of American Liberty."

It was also the great-grandfather of the First Amendment.

That may be a bit too much; while John Peter Zenger did make a tremendous contribution to the freedom of speech and press which we all cherish, he wasn't the originator of the idea. As organist in his Dutch church, he may have heard a sermon or two on the prophet Amos, or his good wife Anna Catherina may have told him about this rebellious and fiery country shepherd who spoke for God against a king and a government and was told to shut up and get out, to go preach somewhere else, and stop stirring up the people. Or he may have known about the John and Peter who were hauled into court for speaking too freely in the streets about a certain Nazarene and were commanded by the court ". . . not to speak at all, nor teach in the name of Jesus" (Acts

4:18). Fortunately for us, these free speakers refused to cease and desist in their reaching for the truth.

> **I believe in free speech** because it is a Bible-based right of men—everywhere in the world and particularly in America.
>
> **I believe in free speech** because I believe that truth is found in free and open discussion.
>
> **I believe in free speech** and a free press because I believe that without free speech no search for truth is possible.
>
> **I believe in free speech** and a free press because I believe that without it our democracy would perish.
>
> **I believe in free speech** in the church because I think a Christian has a right to pick and choose among the creeds and believe what his soul tells him to believe.
>
> **I agree heartily** with the statement in the Constitution of the State of Pennsylvania that "Every citizen may freely speak, write or print on any subject, *being responsible for that liberty*" (italics mine).
>
> And believe it or not, I even believe in letting fools speak their minds.

Maybe I should explain that, before you throw this book out of the window.

Woodrow Wilson was one of the most fiercely criticized and ridiculed presidents we have ever had. He took it gracefully; he knew that this was one of the penalties of being president. He said, "I have always been among those who believed that the greatest freedom of speech was the greatest safety, because if a man is a fool, the best thing to do is to encourage him to advertise the fact by speaking. It cannot be so easily discovered if you allow him to remain silent and look wise, but if you let him speak, the secret is out and the world knows that he is a fool."

Take, for instance, the case of Archie Bunker on the TV show "All in the Family." To many people, he is so repulsive that they refuse to watch the show or listen to his nonsense. As Carroll O'Connor plays him, Archie takes the prize as being the American Least Likely to Be Admired. His language is ear-splitting; his frequent references to Niggers, Wops, Chinks and Micks, and some of his almost blasphemous references to God infuriate us. But his show is at the top of the TV broadcasts *because he is making us laugh.* Archie is played as an idiot—an arrogant, bigoted, illiterate, uneducated, illogical, ill-mannered, ill-tempered, ridiculous fool. And when a man is a fool he invites laughter at himself and at everything he says. The bigot is a fool, and his foolishness only makes the good sense of the truth more evident and desirable. We may even *need* fools, at times, to remind us that we ourselves are sometimes sinful and stupid in thinking that *our* voice is the only voice of God!

Much as I disagree with a lot that Archie says, I would let him speak. I haven't much respect for fools, but I am old enough to know that sometimes fools speak wisely.

There is a good story about Roger Williams sailing on a ship with a fellow passenger who was constantly telling everybody that the ship was heading for a deadly reef —straight ahead. He said it so often, and in such ludicrous tones, that the passengers—and even the captain—finally told him to keep quiet. Some of them even proposed that they throw him overboard. They never got the chance to do that, for the vessel suddenly hit the reef and sank. Said Roger Williams, "They had drowned the giver of the warning, but the reef remained."

But this has its limits; we cannot put too much confidence in the counsel of fools. That can and often does encourage a free speech that is as dangerous as a copperhead let loose in a schoolroom. Wise old Justice Holmes once remarked that no one has the right to yell *fire* in a crowded theater. Too much free speech can be destructive to the very rights it pretends to defend. What this country needs, says another sage, is more free speech worth listening to.

Uncontrolled free speech can stimulate crime. What crimes have been committed in the name of liberty! Napoleon talked a lot about liberty, equality, and fraternity, while he was bathing Europe in a bloodbath to satisfy his own ego and ambition—and he *didn't* do very much to establish liberty, equality, and fraternity. The irony of his hypocrisy was demonstrated by one of his marshals who addressed the people in one country he had conquered in these words, "We have come to bring you liberty and equality, but don't let that go to your heads, for the first one who makes a move without my permission will be shot." That sounds like the "liberation" of Communism! (Did you know that the people of the Union of Soviet Socialist Republics are "guaranteed by law, freedom of speech, freedom of the press, freedom of assembly, and freedom of street demonstration?" What a dirty lie *that* is!)

I do *not* believe in any anarchial, purely destructive freedom of speech that is used as an excuse for violence.

Our son, Dusty, told me recently that he had heard a comic say on television, "Our Constitution is a joke." To me, that comedian's material, as such, is not funny; it's sick. Our Constitution a joke? What kind of irresponsible drivel is this, on the part of a so-called comic who would never have had the chance to say a thing like that without the provisions of the First Amendment? If this is freedom of speech, you can have it; I despise it.

I haven't much use either, for the wild-eyed left-wingers who parade in the street carrying the Stars and Stripes and yelling for the destruction of everything that the Stars and Stripes stand for. They spit on the flag, and they even burn it. They break every law in the books and then, when they come into court, plead for their constitutional rights! Then the Constitution is not only a joke, but a defense of disloyalty.

I believe in the right of dissent—*with respect.* The insulting and sometimes libelous remarks of some of the "stand-up" comics on television about our government and government officials is in incredibly bad taste and detrimental to our national image.

I believe in free speech, but I do not like to see it abused in a pornography that is repulsive to any healthy, decent mind. Eddie Cantor said once that when a comic had to depend on dirty stories for applause, he ought to get off the stage and stay off. Right on, Eddie! I do not believe that any comic or any media has any moral right to enter my living room with shows built on sheer violence, sex, and profanity so rotten that they have to advise us parents that perhaps the children shouldn't see it. Well, what is wrong for my kids is wrong for me.

Look at the "nudie" magazines on the newsstands—or at the movie ads in the newspapers. I counted them up in just one newspaper, for one day, and I found that 80 to 90 percent of the ads were marked $X$ or FOR ADULTS ONLY. If they are bad for the children, what makes them good for *us?* These days adultery is flaunted on page 1. They boast of children out of wedlock, and they produce pictures that are not fit to be shown at a smoker.

Or I walk into a bookstore and find that I have to fight my way through the dirty book section, replete with books by professional prostitutes, before I can find a book I'd want to leave out on my living-room table. Has true creativity in books and films all but disappeared in this avalanche of lewd thinking? The authors and publishers rant about "art" in these books and films. What "art" is there in pornography? Of what good is dirt for dirt's sake? Of what value is profanity (the sign of a limited vocabulary)? It isn't smart, or even good *avant-garde:* it is pathetic. Has imagination departed our minds? Is there no room, anymore, for the nuance, the subtle suggestion in writing and film production? Have we, like the old Romans, become so jaded in our appetites that we can no longer appreciate delicacy?

We have no right to use freedom of speech as a license for corruption. Freedom and license, you know, are two quite different things. You can't excuse it—as some are trying to—on the ground that we humans are mere animals "with a higher intelligence." Well, if all this is higher intelligence, may God have mercy upon us! We are not behaving like intelligent human beings; we are behaving like animals who follow only their animalistic instincts. *We* have been endowed by the Creator with the ability to know right from wrong and purity from muck, and with a sensitivity of soul. Judging by the present trend, we are obviously unappreciative of these special gifts.

My Bible tells me, in Proverbs 15:4: "A wholesome tongue is a tree of life: but perverseness therein is a breach in the spirit." And Proverbs 18:21 tells me something about speech, free and otherwise: "Death and life are in the power of the tongue: and they that love it shall eat of the fruit thereof." Let us beware of an unruly tongue or pen; we may just reap what we have sown by our rash words. The tongue has destroyed many lives, reputations, ideals, and ambitions. And Matthew caps it all with this:

> A good man out of the good treasure of the heart bringeth forth good things: and an evil man out of the evil treasure bringeth forth evil things. But I say unto you, That every idle

word that men shall speak, they shall give account thereof in the day of judgment. For by
thy words thou shalt be justified, and by thy
words thou shalt be condemned.

Matthew 12:35–37

I plead guilty to having used too many "idle" words
—of speaking before thinking because I have the right to
speak. Were it not for these words of Christ, I would be
lost and desperate to know what to say and how and when
to say it. I know well, as James knew, that "If any man
among you seem to be religious, and bridleth not his
tongue . . . this man's religion is vain" (1:26).

I need to read this Scripture every day of my life; I
need to apply it before I speak on anything, lest my
religion—and my devotion to my country—become vain
and hypocritical.

I pray: "Oh, God, Thou hast given me my tongue and
the right to use it; may I use it well, for Thee, and never
for anything or anyone less than Thee."

# 6

# Freedom of Worship

In our country, we are proud of the Pilgrims and the Puritans—and we should be proud. We remember them lovingly on Thanksgiving Day; we have honored them in statues and in paintings and in church and in school-books. Occasionally we smile at them and even ridicule them:

> . . . the old three-cornered hat,
> And the breeches, and all that. . . .

but in our hearts we love them:

> O beautiful for pilgrim feet,
> Whose stern, impassioned stress
> A thoroughfare for freedom beat
> Across the wilderness!

"The Puritan," said philosopher David Hume, "was the only man in the seventeenth century who dared stand up and fight for liberty."

But (I may lose a few friends and influence nobody by what I say here, but please hear me through), much as we love him as a gallant fighter for religious freedom, we must remember that while the men of Plymouth and the Bay Colony didn't want anyone to tell *them* how to worship, they wanted to tell *others* how to worship. They imposed restrictions on others and threw those who were not of their belief into jail; they hanged a little Quaker woman, Mary Dyer, on Boston Common, and they drove Roger Williams into a winter wilderness.

The truth is that there was no real religious *freedom* in any of the American colonies for more than a century. Even in Pennsylvania, Catholics could not hold public office and certain political privileges were limited to Christians; even in Rhode Island, there were civil disabilities inflicted on Jews and Catholics, in spite of Roger Williams. There was not even a tolerance of religious worship until the time of the Revolution—and there is a vast difference between tolerance and freedom.

The first real blow for freedom of worship was struck in Virginia in 1776, in what we know as the Virginia Bill of Rights, in which it was laid down that "All men are equally entitled to the full and free exercise of religion according to the dictates of conscience; and that it is the natural duty of all to practice Christian forbearance, love and charity toward each other . . . . No man, or class of men, ought on account of religion to be invested with peculiar emoluments or privileges, or subjected to any penalties or disabilities . . . ."

George Mason wrote the original which was later copied into the Constitution by Thomas Jefferson. From that moment on, Congress had no right, under the law, to prohibit the "free exercise of religion."

The Pilgrims and the Puritans were genuine and courageous pioneers of the freedom of worship which developed in the United States after they were gone. We shouldn't expect a few settlers in Massachusetts to do it all and at once—*but they started it.*

They came here with the conviction that without faith in God there can be no true freedom or any truly free nation; they believed with all their hearts that where there is no vision the people perish, and that any nation that builds upon anything but an awareness of God is built on shifting sand. They sowed the seed, and left it to future generations to see it blossom into full flower in our Constitution.

I often hear someone say that there is something

wrong with the Constitution because it doesn't mention the name of God. No, it doesn't—but I say the Constitution is God-based, whether God's name is mentioned or not. It came to life, as we have already said, in prayer; it set the people of the Church free from persecution by the State for preaching and teaching their convictions about God. Thanks to the Constitution, we have a great Principle of Separation of Church and State written into the law of the land.

I think we should keep that, but—excuse me for rocking the boat a bit, will you?—I often wonder if we don't sometimes go too far in our efforts to separate Church and State—so far that we tend to forget that we the people *are* the Church and that, if you don't mind, we'd like to keep it that way. We must, as Mahalia Jackson used to sing, "Let the Church roll on . . ." if we are to remain a free nation, and we cannot allow the influence of the Church upon the State to diminish. *The Church is the conscience of the State.* I say that you cannot and should not separate religious belief and religious conscience completely from the State, when it was belief in Almighty God and freedom under Him that founded the State! There is a Divine Authority involved here that is higher than the authority of the State and to which we owe our first allegiance! the Omnipotent, Omniscient, Omnipresent God who is the Light of every man who comes into the world.

To me, the idea of divorcing God from our national life is insulting to God. President Lyndon Johnson, in a crucial hour in our history, reminded us that above the pyramid on the great seal of the United States, it says in Latin (translated), GOD HAS FAVORED OUR UNDERTAKING. I cannot believe God will very long favor any government or any nation which denies His existence in their midst. William McLaughlin and Robert N. Ballah expressed it well in a book entitled *Religion in America:*

> . . . Religion is not something that comes to a man from an . . . institution that possesses and communicates grace; rather, the institution is formed by the voluntary association in fellowship of religious people. In this characteristic, America clearly shows the dominance of the free-church tradition over its religious life. This emphasis in turn explains the kind of unity between the secular and the religious that has been achieved in America . . . .

In other words, the governmental institution in our country did not give us religious freedom; it was concern for such freedom under God that gave us our free government! We just cannot separate the two.

So, in the name of religious freedom, I still believe in teaching children to bow their heads in public schools in prayer to God. I realize that many of my readers may not agree with that, but I do, and that's that. I think it wrong that one atheistic woman in this country should be allowed to stop prayer in the schools. She may be defending "the right to be an atheist," but it seems to me that those of us who believe in God have some rights, too. If some of our children are the children of atheistic parents, let them simply quiet their minds for a few moments before launching into their studies. Children who believe in God and are taught to believe in God in their homes have just as much "right" as the children of atheists. Our concept of freedom is freedom *under* God, not *from* Him.

The atheists and the agnostics are quite right in calling their assemblages a "church," for they most surely have an idol of worship—namely, themselves. But this country and its standards of freedom were not founded by men who worshiped themselves. They worshiped God, and that's why we are free to worship Him—and why the atheists are free to express their convictions. But does a handful of atheists have the right to override the desire of Christian people to express *their* convictions and desires? I don't get it—at all!

I also believe that it is good to have religious services and prayer groups and Bible-study groups in the White House, if the White House wants it. Is the White House not the home of the president of the United States, as well as our national State House? It is more than just a tax-supported institutional building; it is the sanctuary of a man who carries the tremendous burden of the nation's highest office. Where can any man go, under such stress, but to God? Abraham Lincoln said once, in the days when he seemed to be losing a war, "In these terrible days, I am often driven to my knees because I have nowhere else to go." That was a religious service with two participating: the president and God.

The presidency is a fearful responsibility borne by one man, and it is the loneliest post in the world. Because the president holds a prayer meeting or a religious service in his house does not mean that he is ordering anyone to worship or not to worship; he isn't demanding that anyone come to such a service. No one condemns him for holding musical concerts, or dinners for diplomats or friends. Why condemn the religious service? Such services are easily justified, provided, of course, that they are for inspirational purposes, and not political maneuvers.

It all boils down to this: shall we as a nation worship the Creator or the creature? Shall our moral and spiritual standards be the mere whims of one man, or the serious judgments of consecrated, God-fearing men?

Yes, I know—we had Watergate while prayer meetings were being held in the White House. That was a shameful performance—but wasn't it shameful because this little group of men highly placed put more faith in their power than in the power of God? It wasn't only these men who did that: We all fell far short of the Kingdom's rules when we shrugged our shoulders and said, "Oh, everybody does it!" We all seemed to have forgotten that morality cannot be maintained without true religion. No less a consecrated president than George Washington warned us that we cannot expect that "National morality can prevail in exclusion of religious principle." And President Kennedy expressed the same principle when he said, at his inauguration, ". . . Let us go forth to lead the land we love, asking His blessing and His help, but knowing that here on earth God's work must truly be our own." *Amen!*

Yes—we do seem to have gone overboard, morally, in this generation—and we have done our best to sweep this fact under the rug. But I am afraid that this idea of "going about our business as usual," no matter how rotten that business may be, isn't going to get the job done if we want to advance upward and not downward in our great democracy. The biblical admonition, "Choose you this day whom ye will serve  . . ." (Joshua 24:15) applies to all of us, in and beyond the White House. God's Word is timeless, for all of us. So let us not allow the heart of America to crystalize further in materialistic godlessness; let us turn from our wicked ways, repent, and ask God to heal our land.

To cover the sin in one's life (or in national life) by attempting to assuage the pain of a burning conscience in applying the oil of the so-called "new morality" is like taking aspirin for cancer. The cancer can be surgically removed or treated medically, or miraculously removed by the healing touch of the Great Physician. Unconfessed or accumulated sin becomes cancerous to the soul. There is only One who can cure it, and His name is Jesus. I speak from experience. I am one with the man who was cured of blindness by his Lord, and who shouted, "All I know is whereas I was once blind, now I see!" (Read about this in John 9:25.) No amount of philosophy, self-hypnosis or any of the do-it-yourself kits for psyching yourself into a rationalizing of wrongdoing will get the job done. How I tried that year after year! Not until I went back to the "old-time religion" of throwing my-self on the mercy of God through Christ, did I experience forgiveness, peace, and joy in my heart—and real purpose for my life. When you hear me sing "Give me that old-time religion" you can bet your life I mean it!

Not long ago, the Variety Clubs of America hosted a banquet to honor Billy Graham. Now the Variety Clubs is a show-business venture to help needy children and adults. While I am sure that the majority of the guests at the banquet were not Christians in the strict sense of the word, certainly the purpose of the occasion was Christian. Billy said to them, "Get into the Word of God deeply, for we are facing difficult times . . . ." Bill Bright (of Campus Crusade for Christ) said that in his travels all over the world, he had gotten the impression from political leaders, academic leaders in colleges and universities, and from many preachers in outstanding churches, that the picture was very dark, indeed, and that all of us should be spending our money *now* on spreading the Gospel of Christ. The intimation was —and truly is—that the day may not be far off when we will be denied the privilege of supporting our free churches and worshiping freely in them—a day when we will have no Bibles to read.

That sounds rather awesome, doesn't it? It is that —and it is a challenge to the Church in America to get back to its main purpose—the spreading of the Gospel of *freedom in Christ* across the whole world. It reminds us of the words of Malachi.

. . . You have robbed me of the tithes and offerings due to me. And so the awsome curse of God is cursing you, for your whole nation has been robbing me. Bring all the tithes into the storehouse so that there will be food enough in my Temple; if you do, I will open up the windows of heaven for you and pour out a blessing so great you won't have room enough to take it in! . . . And all nations will call you blessed, for you will be a land sparkling with happiness. These are the promises of the Lord of Hosts.

Malachi 3:8–10; 12 LB

Now the Bible tells us to "Occupy until the Lord comes again." (*See* Luke 19:13.) I put a lot of emphasis on that word *occupy,* for to me I believe we should occupy as Christians until our Lord returns, regardless of hardship, deprivation, persecution—whatever. *Occupy* means *to live our Christianity,* to fill our place right where we are day by day, hour by hour, minute by minute. It means for us to take a stand for whatever the Lord God tells us is right in His sight. It means to take ridicule without rancor, loss without bitterness, plaudits with humility, and blessings with thanksgiving. It means to do the task —however menial or great—as unto Him, not being slothful but alive and ready. It means to pray, to be in communication with Him at all times, to be on constant speaking terms with Him, and to listen to and follow the promptings of His voice within us even when it means personal sacrifice. Too hard? Read the lives of the apostles! Read of the sacrifices of our forefathers! Had they not sacrificed for future generations, where would we be today?

Yes, I know there are dangers involved in all this. We must be careful not to *impose* this freedom in Christ anywhere upon anyone. Carlyle wrote, once, that "No iron chain, or outward force of any kind, could ever compel the soul of man to believe or disbelieve." We must not force it, like the American who said to a group of South Sea Islanders, "I'll make this country a democracy, if I have to kill every one of you!" Not that. It must be done in love and in a teaching of the truth of God. There is such a thing as too much freedom; we've no right to abuse it, or overdo it. There are some things I don't believe about freedom of worship, and this is one of them.

Neither do I believe that we have any right to ignore the religious rights of others who may differ from us in their worship.

I do not believe that religious freedom entitles us to do or say anything we please in the name of that freedom —like running naked in the streets, as one sect once did in old New England, or causing confusion and disrupting a church service.

I don't believe any of us have any right to disobey the country's law. (The Mormons once practiced polygamy; they stopped that practice when it was made a violation of federal law.)

When Emma Lazarus wrote that immortal line,

"Yearning to breathe free . . ." for the Statue of Liberty, she wasn't referring to any such trivial and abusive freedom as this. She had something higher in mind; she was referring us back to that great spiritual heritage of America which has made us what we are. She believed, with many of us, that God had a hand in the making of this land, and that in God lies the strength and beauty of America. We believe in this country that man was created in the image of God, and that man was set free through the will of God—*and that we should never, never forget that.*

Richard M. DeVos, a church elder and president of AMWAY, a multimillion-dollar enterprise, says this in a newly published book called *Believe!*

> Perhaps the man who has summed it up best was Carlos Romulo, soldier, statesman and Philippine patriot, who served with General Douglas MacArthur in World War II and played a leading role in creating the United Nations. He was the Philippine ambassador to this country for some years, and a former president of the UN General Assembly. When he left America for the last time, he said. this:

> I am going home, America—farewell. For seventeen years, I have enjoyed your hospitality, visited every one of your fifty states. I can say I know you well, I admire and love America. It is my second home. What I have to say now in parting is both a tribute and a warning. Never forget, Americans, that yours is a spiritual country. Yes, I know that

you are a practical people. Like others, I have mar-
veled at your factories, your skyscrapers and
your arsenals. But underlying everything else is the
fact that America began as a God-loving, God-
fearing, God-worshiping people, knowing that
there is a spark of the Divine in each one of us. It is
this respect for the dignity of the human spirit
which makes America invincible. May it always en-
dure.

And so I say again in parting, thank you,
America, and farewell. May God keep you always
—and may you always keep God.

That says it!

# 7

# Freedom From Want

President Roosevelt's third freedom was *freedom from want*. This word *want* is a tricky one. It means different things to different people—anything from plain greed to food that will mean the difference between life and death.

We begin *wanting* the minute we begin to live—in the cradle. Listen to that baby cry! He's hungry, and he yells his head off until he is fed. As a young child, his most familiar line is, "Mommy, I want, I want, I want." He usually gets what he wants, and the more he is given, the more he seems to want. And if we are foolish enough to give him *everything* he wants, we find ourselves with a spoiled child on our hands. We aren't happy about that, and neither is the child happy about it, for he soon finds out that *some* of his wants can be greedy and harmful. But he keeps at it; he never has enough to satisfy him. Eventually, he has little respect for the parents who give him everything. It is a stupid performance. Should we give the growing child food that will stunt his growth, just because he thinks he wants it? Or a cigarette to a seven year old? *Wanting* can be a death warrant!

The same thing holds true with the grown-up child. The more we have, the more we want, and after a while, nothing satisfies us. Someone asked the old millionaire, J. P. Morgan, when a millionaire was satisfied that he had millions enough. He replied, "When he makes the next one!" Those who fail to make "the big money" turn bitter; they have all they *need*, but they want more, more, more. The man next door buys a Chevy; we must buy a Buick. We come to Christmas, and we knock ourselves out trying to find something to give a friend who "has everything" and end up giving him a lot of junk he doesn't want at all—insulting the One who was born with nothing, in a Bethlehem stable.

What a hideous world this would be if everyone got everything he wants! Jesus was thinking of this when He said:

> Don't store up treasures here on earth where they can erode away or may be stolen. Store them in heaven where they will never lose their value, and are safe from thieves. If your profits are in heaven your heart will be there too.
>
> Matthew 6:19–21 LB

Now we in America have all we need—and a lot more. We are the richest nation on earth—and our lust for yet more riches has made us what other, poorer nations call a "materialistic" nation. I notice that many of these poorer nations do not hesitate to ask us for money (and then despise us for giving it!) but that is beside the point. The point is that our society *has* become enslaved to its materialistic wants. How do we free ourselves from that?

First, I believe that it must begin with our mortal bodies. To do that we must look beyond ourselves to our Creator. You and I must remember that He knows what we *need* for our spiritual, mental, and physical well-being. I must submit my wants to Him, and be willing to wait for an answer—meanwhile performing the obvious tasks at hand, knowing that He will supply my need according to His riches in Christ Jesus.

It sounds odd, but many people who are called "poverty-stricken" are actually happy, and some others

who are called rich are unhappy. My morning newspaper tells me about a rich man who lost his mind, then
lost his money—and murdered his whole family! The
so-called happy poor that I speak of have their treasure
in heaven, not in Wall Street. An abundance of things
does not necessarily spell out happiness. Indeed, the
more money and material things we have, the greater is
the responsibility of stewardship, and the greater the
necessity of guarding against others who would like to
get a piece of it, by hook or by crook. "Of him to whom
much is given, much shall be required." (*See* Luke 12:48.)
Right?

Freedom from want involves fairness on the part of
those who have and those who have not. Freedom from
want demands prudence in handling what is there—not
in being penurious but prudent in spending, in saving,
and goodwill, in giving to others who have less. Freedom
from want implies working for your daily bread, being
industrious, being glad of the opportunity to serve in
return for payment—not in sitting down with an out-
stretched hand when one is mentally and physically able
to work. I believe in being interested in the welfare of my
brothers and sisters, but I am a bit fed up with a "welfare"
that has become a racket in our country on the part of
those who are fit to work and refuse to work. Grand-
fathers and grandsons alike live on money scrounged
from those who *do* work. I am also fed up with labor
organizations that demand more, more, more when the
national economy is almost in a state of disaster, and with
certain managements who use the same moment of disas-

ter to skyrocket prices and profits, robbing every house-wife and wage earner in the country. I believe with all my heart in free enterprise; but I don't like to see it abused, and I don't like being "took."

Yet, in spite of all this abuse, I still believe that freedom means *giving*—the giving of our bounties, the giving of ourselves. "Ask, and it shall be given you," said Jesus, "seek and ye shall find" (Matthew 7:7). He also taught us the value of work and of using our God-given talents and abilities for the good of all, not just for our own prosperity. He taught the rewards of free enterprise. (Read the Parable of the Talents in Matthew 25:15–30.) And He made it clear that if we honestly want to be free of want in our lives, we must diligently seek the will of God in our living. It is according to His will that we are supplied with what He deems necessary. The Bible says that "The cattle on a thousand hills are mine (*see* Psalms 50:10)—God's. If we acknowledge Him as Father and as the Source to supply all our needs, He will see that we get enough. As for those who ignore God and His admonitions, those who greedily grab and tenaciously hold another's rightful share, they shall get their just desserts. "He that oppresseth the poor reproacheth his Maker: but he that honoureth him hath mercy on the poor" (Proverbs 14:31).

I can just hear, right now, some good reader saying, "So Dale Evans is an authority on economics!" No, I'm not. I am no economist; the perplexities and problems involved in economics baffle me, just as they seem to baffle and disturb the most skilled economists in the high seats of government. I have great sympathy for them;

they deal with seemingly unsolvable problems —problems almost too enmeshed and entangled to be unraveled. I still have hope in them—and even more hope in a God who, my Bible tells me, will make our crooked ways straight. (*See* Isaiah 40:4.) *And I believe that He must have our help in doing that.* It has to start with God, you, and me!

Let's take a look at our economic situation.

When Franklin D. Roosevelt spoke of freedom from want, he was certainly speaking of *human hunger* and *poverty.* He pioneered in what we have come to call "the war on poverty"—a just war, if there ever was one—and the presidents who succeeded him have picked up the torch and carried on the war. They fought it not just for us, but for all the world.

Up to this point, I have been writing about general principles. Now let's get specific about it.

Not very many Americans believe that we have a "want" problem in this country. We have enough to eat, so we pay too little attention to those who haven't enough. The truth is, we have a poverty of which we should be heartily ashamed. On TV the other night, a man who runs a delicatessen in New York City said that he had an elderly couple who were buying quantities of dog food—and he knew that they hadn't a dog in their house for twenty years.

It's that kind of hidden poverty—hidden, like cancer. We don't know about it because we don't *see* it, but it's there. A report of a Select Senate Committee this past year said this: "In a nation in which the wealthiest 1

percent possess more than eight times the wealth of the
bottom 50 percent, in which the percentage of national
income going to the lowest fifth of the population has
remained the same for 45 years, and in which 40 million
people remain poor or near-poor, more than a food
stamp or child-feeding program is at issue . . . ."
Something more. Could it be that our Christian conscience and Christian concern for the poor has fallen fast
asleep?

Oh, we say, sure, we have *some* poverty in our over-
crowded cities; we should *expect* that. Didn't Jesus say,
"The poor always ye have with you" (John 12:8)? When
you get a lot of undereducated and underprivileged and
underskilled people huddled together in one place, you
are bound to have poverty.

But it isn't that way, at all! Poverty in the United States
is rural as well as it is urban. A report by Gordon
Cavanaugh, executive director of the Housing Assist-
ance Council to a Senate Committee, said that "The
approximately 11½ million rural citizens living in substandard housing in this country is equivalent to the total
population of the state of Pennsylvania. . . . I spent
six years directing the housing and food programs in one
of the country's largest cities and, along with many, I
would not have believed that the dreadful conditions in
many urban areas did not represent the bulk of our
nation's shelter problems. I was wrong. *There is an American subcontinent of substandard housing, and it is rural
America.*" (Italics mine.)

Have we forgotten the Jesus who spent so much if not

most of His time on earth with and for the poor, and who
left us with this word of rebuke:

> For I was hungry, and you gave me no food, I
> was thirsty and you gave me no drink, I was a
> stranger and you did not welcome me, naked
> and you did not clothe me.
>
> Matthew 25:42, 43

Have we forgotten the prophet Amos who cried out
against the hypocritical rich in protest—against the rich
who gorged themselves on feast days while the poor went
hungry? Amos declared, "I hate, I despise your feast
days . . ." (5:21).

I know that basically the American people are a chari-
table people at heart, and a generous people by reputation. That Canadian commentator who came to the defense of the United States in a broadcast that shook up
both Canadians and Americans told the world that he
could name "five thousand times when the Americans
raced to help other people in trouble. Can you name me
even one time when someone else raced to the Americans
in trouble?" He's right. We have been generous—within
certain limits. Much as we have given across the whole
world to stave off famine and relieve the suffering poor,
we haven't even scratched the surface of what we might
and *should* do. We have given out of our rich bounty—so
little that we didn't even miss it. We have tremendous
resources of wheat and corn and meat (cattle) that could
and should be shared with the poor living both here and

abroad, and yet we read of crops being plowed underground because "we have an overabundance" of such crops. We see pictures of great piles of grain left rotting in the sun.

One of the most horrible pictures I have ever seen was the one showing some farmers in our Midwest shooting their calves because they were going to lose money on them—at the very moment when thousands of adults and children were starving to death in Bangladesh. (Some farmers, thank God, condemned these thoughtless men by sending *their* own calves to relieve the hungry.)

One way to bring about freedom from want was instituted back in the Old Testament days by a statesman named Joseph, who looked at the periodic famines that plagued Egypt, and came up with a great idea: Why not store up the surplus grain (corn) that was reaped in the years of plenty in storehouses or "perpetual granaries" so that the people would not starve in the lean, famine years, "that the land perish not through the famine" (Genesis 41:36). In spite of all our progress since Joseph died, we haven't caught up with him yet, or shown the good common sense to do that! (I know of one group of Americans that does just that; it is said that "No Mormon ever goes hungry"—because the Mormons have just such perpetual granaries!)

This is pure economics—in which, as I have confessed, I am no authority. But I don't have to be an authority, or an expert, to see the wisdom of Joseph's plan. He was smart enough never to tell his people to destroy in order

to keep commerce going through created shortages
which would bring incredibly high prices for the majority
of consumers (while it lined the pockets of the few "on
top"). Joseph found a better way to strike a balance
between the grower and the consumer, which shouldn't
be impossible to *us* to find, *provided we as individuals want to
find it.*

There's the rub—the trouble. As individuals, we would
never turn away a hungry man from our door, or refuse
to give drink to a man dying of thirst in the desert. But
few of us have hungry men pounding on our door these
days, and fewer ever travel in the desert, so we just forget
about all that. I'd like to add something to Joseph's formula for freedom from want—something *personal*—that
only the concerned and Christian person can do, for I
believe that the ultimate remedy for want lies in personal
sacrifice on the part of all of us.

I quote now from a speech made by Senator Mark
Hatfield, at a meeting of the Conservative Baptist Convention in St. Paul, Minnesota. The senator, who is one of
our most beloved statesman in Washington, offers a
specific plan with which I heartily agree.

> Thomas Merton has written, "It is easy
> enough to tell the poor to accept their poverty
> as God's will when you yourself have warm
> clothes and plenty of food and medical care
> and a roof over your head and no worry about
> the rent. But if you want them to believe you,

try to share some of their poverty and see if you can accept it as God's will for yourself!"

The command and compassion of Christ compels us to respond to the physical and spiritual needs of a hungry world.

What concretely can we do? Let me offer some specific suggestions:

• Every congregation could establish a specific budget amount directed to meeting the needs of starving people in some particular point of the world.

• Christians can be asked to give a specific tithe just for the purpose of relieving hunger; further, we should consider a *graduated* tithe, which increases in its percentage according to the amount of one's income. "From those to whom much has been given, much will be expected."

• We should renew the Christian discipline of fasting as a means for teaching us how to identify with those who hunger, and to deepen our life of prayer for those who suffer.

• We must all analyze, in prayer before God, our own habits of food consumption. Specifically, we can drastically alter our consumption of meat, and the money we save we can give to alleviate hunger. Some Christians may decide that part of their witness means being a vegetarian. Families can decide how to limit their consumption of beef, perhaps to only certain days, or as times of special celebration, or just on certain days of the week.

● Next Thanksgiving can be a time when Christians throughout the land join to express their thanksgiving for our plenty, not by a feast, but by a sacrificial outpouring and sharing of our plenty with the needy, as the Pilgrims shared with the Indians.

● As Christians, we can, by our word and our living example, call the nation to the task of sharing from its plenty with those who are in need. (Reprinted from *The Wittenburg Door.*)

That's what I'd call getting down to the nittty-gritty of the whole business of freedom from want. Some of us may say to ourselves, as we read it, "Yeah, that's a good idea, but I doubt that it would work." Of course it won't work, if we don't even try to make it work! But try it or not, *this is putting the Gospel to work,* practicing what we preach, and practicing what Jesus preached. Jesus Christ fed the body as well as the soul. When He found five thousand people hungry, He fed them. He had compassion on the hungry, and He left orders for us to feed the hungry, give drink to the thirsty, clothe the naked, show love to the stranger and the sick, and visit those in prison. (*See* Matthew 25:35–40.) That was not just a good idea; it was a divine *command,* and unless we obey it, we are "none of Him."

Dr. Frank Mead tells about a recent trip to Mexico. He sat with a friend on the porch of a luxurious hotel, looking out over the rooftops of a nearby slum. They had just had a gourmet dinner—one of those meals fit for a king. His friend turned to him and said, "Do you realize that while we were eating this highly expensive dinner in this palace, there were people down there who hardly have a crust of bread to eat? We couldn't even eat all of it—we sent a lot of it back to the kitchen, while those paupers down there . . . ." (A restaurateur of a swank cafe in New York City said the other day that 25 percent of the food served to his customers remained uneaten, and ended up in the garbage pails!)

Yes, that's the trouble; that's the obstacle to freedom from want. We just don't think enough of those who have less than we have. In our conscious or unconscious neglect of those who are in want, we are refusing to admit that we *are* our brothers' keepers.

*Gimme, gimme, gimme* is the name of the game. Gimme wealth, gimme a Cadillac, gimme the best food, gimme the best clothes, gimme, gimme, gimme. "I know—there are a lot of poor people and I feel sorry for them, and I'll give what I can . . . ." *But we don't give what we can.* We give what we won't miss. We to whom God has given so much, give so little! If we gave everything we have we still could not outgive God.

On the tombstone of Christopher Chapman in Westminster Abbey, bearing the date 1680, there is an inscription that stops everyone who sees it. It reads:

WHAT I GAVE, I HAVE,
WHAT I SPENT, I HAD,
WHAT I LEFT, I LOST.
BY NOT GIVING IT.

The Bible asks in Psalms 8:4, "What is man, that thou
art mindful of him? and the son of man, that thou visitest
him?" Everything man has belongs to God; all Creation is
His. In the Second Psalm, we are asked, "Why do the
heathen rage, and the people imagine a vain thing? The
kings of the earth set themselves, and the rulers take
counsel together, against the Lord, and against his
anointed, saying, Let us break their bands asunder, and
cast away their cords from us. He that sitteth in the
heavens shall laugh: the Lord shall have them in deri-
sion." It would be well for us to memorize that whole
psalm, for it speaks to us of our condition. We have lost
our vision of the creative power of Almighty God and of
the healing compassion of Jesus Christ His Son.

When Roy and I first started paying tribute to God and
country in our shows, some folks criticized us for "inject-
ing a religious element." Many of them in high, strategic
places of public communication would accuse us of
"preaching" and of "using our religion for commercial
purposes." But there has been a change in all that, and
the criticism has died away. Today many others besides
ourselves are speaking out for God and country, in the
world of entertainment and on TV and radio. They are
finding a highly receptive audience, for the people of this

country have found out that *as a nation, we are groping in moral and economic chaos.* And they want help, to bring order out of that chaos—a help that can come not out of human experiments in economics, not out of any great political program of reform, but out of a fresh allegiance to the will and way and power of God to change all things and to bring forth all that is good.

As we approach the two-hundred-year mark in our splendid democracy within a republic, may we lift our eyes to the hills of the future, knowing that our help cometh from the Lord who made heaven and earth and who inspired democracy. May we not be slack in our promises to those coming after us, to keep the torch of freedom burning brightly within our hearts, and doing all we can to keep it lighted in the hearts of our young. Let us "train up a child in the way he shall go," with full assurance that when he is old he will not forget it, but, in turn, train his children so. Jesus said, "Heaven and earth shall pass away: but my words shall not pass away" (Mark 13:31).

I believe it. Do you?

Freedom from want! Every decent-minded, Christ-minded Christian wants it—and every Christian so minded has to realize that there are some other tremendous "wants" that lie under the surface of freedom from the hunger of poverty.

*We are hungry* for God; we will never satisfy that hunger until we—*we*—turn to Him in spirit and in truth and penitence and commitment.

*We are hungry* for peace; we will never get it until we are at peace with Him, and start living in love and not by the sword.

*We are hungry* for beauty in our dirty world; we will never get it until we come to Him in the beauty of holiness.

*We are hungry* for love; we will never get that until we learn to love our brothers as God loves us. People living in slums are an insult to the Spirit.

We must not think that our talents are too small to be useful in the needs of so large a world. Jesus wants us to bring them to Him. Indeed, He calls us to participate in sharing—have we forgotten the miracle that fed the multitudes?

God works miracles in whatever *we* have, and uses *our* gifts to feed this hungry world.

God has no hands but *our* hands.

# 8

# Freedom From Fear

You have hardly started to read your Bible when you come across the words, ". . . I was afraid . . . and I hid myself" (Genesis 3:10). That was Adam in Eden, and evidence that fear has been the black plague of the human race ever since the first man tried (in vain) to hide from God.

Then along comes the line in Proverbs 1:7, which tells us that "The fear of the Lord is the beginning of [wisdom]. . . ." This mention of the "fear" of the Lord runs through the whole Bible; at times it means apprehension, fright, or even panic in the face of danger, but in other references it means a feeling of awe, wonder, and reverence in the presence of God or a manifestation of God. The Living Bible paraphrases here: "How does a man become wise? The first step is to trust and reverence the Lord!"

Call it anything you please—*awesomeness, reverence,* or just plain *fear,* the truth remains that a holy, humble fear of the Almighty will help us to be free from the tyranny of man. Fear is not always bad; it can be a wholesome, constructive thing. But more about that later.

Now when President Roosevelt spoke of "freedom from fear" he was speaking not of reverence for God but of a paralyzing, frightening terror that has gripped the whole world. We may not admit it, but we are *all* captives in a prison house of international fear. We shudder every time we think of the nuclear bomb; we recall with horror the bomb that was dropped on Hiroshima—and we wonder if and when another such bomb is going to fall on us. Dr. Harold Urey, who was the Nobel prizewinner and one of the physicists whose work led to the atom bomb wrote this: "I write to make you afraid. I, myself, am a man who is afraid. All the wise men I know are afraid." One of the men in the plane that dropped the Hiroshima bomb said, as he watched the explosion below, "Good God, *what have we done?*" Man and not God has created this terror.

We fear the Russians, and we spend unbelievable billions of dollars to keep ahead of them in the arms race. The Russians fear us; Khrushchev said, "We will bury you!" We look at the nations of Africa and fear what could happen if all Africa ever got together and . . . ? We read about action on the Golan Heights, and talk about World War III. We read of what Palestinian terrorists did at the Olympic Games in Munich, and we say it could happen here, if we staged the Olympics in the United States. We are almost in panic at the thought of the Arabs cutting off our oil supply. Bishop Gerald Kennedy summed it up in a sermon:

> We have a fear of the future. Since the Second World War, we have lived in the midst of an atmosphere of hopelessness and dread of tomorrow. The extremists play on this weakness and tell us about our leadership that is contaminated and our society that is subverted . . . . We are in desperate need of men who have faith in our traditions of freedom and confidence in the fundamental decency of American citizens.

It is so true that it hurts. There has come over us a loss of confidence in the American way of economic life; we condemn President Gerald Ford's economic plans before the poor man has a chance to explain them, and we accuse Congress of fumbling the ball before they even begin to discuss laws for relief. We are afraid of each other! (We forget that the American people have faced such crises before, and have always united to overcome them.) Two youngsters in Kensington, Maryland, circulated copies of the Bill of Rights in the Constitution as a petition, and asked 101 of their neighbors to sign it. More than half refused to sign it. One woman said it was unpatriotic!

What has happened to us, anyway? We have turned our backs on the spiritual ideals of the founders of this country—*and on God*. We have forgotten that they based their faith and the hope of their Christian commonwealth on the Pauline dictum that ". . . where the Spirit of the Lord is, there is liberty" (2 Corinthians 3:17).

Away back in 1789, the Connecticut legislature was in session, debating some much-needed legislation. Suddenly, the sun disappeared, and the whole town was caught in a terrifying darkness. People lost their wits, and ran wildly in the streets; the end of the world had come! The lawgivers were almost as bad. One of them got up and said in a trembling voice, "It is the Lord's great day. Let us adjourn."

But one of them—Abraham Davenport—stopped it. He leaped to his feet and said to them, as Whittier records it in his poem:

But be it so or not, I only know
My present duty, and my Lord's command

To occupy till He come.
Where He hath set me in His providence
I choose for one to meet Him face to face.
No faithless servant frightened from his task. . . .

Candles were lighted, and the panic disappeared, and
the business of the legislature was concluded. Whittier
concludes:

> And there he stands in memory to this day
> Erect, self-poised, a rugged face half seen
> Against the background of unnatural light,
> A witness to the ages as they pass,
> That simple duty hath no place for fear.

Read that last line again: "That simple duty hath no
place for fear." We need not fear that God has lost us or
our country; we only need to know that we have lost Him,
and that in common sense we should get back to the
business—the *duty*—of making this country of ours what
He intended it to be. And back to the magnificent conviction of Saint Paul that "If God be for us, who can be
against us?" (Romans 8:31).

Speaking of our Christian duty, our minister, Rev.
William O. Hansen, preached a sermon a few weeks ago
that got under my skin and into my heart, and he has
given me permission to use it in this book. He based the
sermon on the experience of Jesus in the city of Gadara
—and on a bumper sticker in California. He started out
by telling us that he had seen a sticker that said, AMER-

ICA, LOVE IT OR LEAVE IT and he proceeded to compare life in Gadara with life in America. Gadara, he said, was actually a city-state developed by the Greeks. Its urban center was laid out in good geometric pattern that gave maximum flow of traffic. Then governmental, commercial, and religious centers were created, and beyond the core of the city were agricultural zones, made up of rich grainfields and pasturelands watered by an elaborate aqueduct system. Gadara was prosperous, and seemingly a good place in which to live.

As the influence of Greece waned, the Romans came in and the great Roman system of law was added to the philosophy and literature of the Greeks. They also built fine highways which brought more commerce to Gadara. When Jesus visited the city it was a proud and wealthy country and city populated by a people who were quite sure they had achieved "the good life."

But Jesus discovered something about Gadara that its inhabitants had missed—or deliberately neglected. He saw that they were doing a better job of solving their technical problems than they were in solving the problems of human need. In the outskirts of Gadara He found a man living in a cave in the local burial ground—a man who was mad ("possessed of an unclean spirit"). (*See* Mark 5:2–17.) Jesus healed him. "Then went the devils out of the man, and entered into the swine . . ." (a herd of swine feeding nearby). The swine went mad; they rushed down a steep place into a lake and were drowned, while their herdsman stood helpless and outraged at the destruction of his property.

A delegation from the city came out to investigate; they found a man who had been mad sitting now calm and rational. They also saw the dead pigs in the water. And they saw Jesus, who had done what they never even tried to do—who had restored a madman to sanity. We would think that they would have been glad at the sight of the healed man, but no, they were more interested in the pigs! A man's property had been destroyed, and they couldn't stand for that!

They were good men—civilized men—in that delegation. They didn't stone Jesus or beat Him. They simply, politely, and firmly, told Him to get out of their country and stay out. He had disturbed the peace of the good life of Gadara. He had challenged that. Their first concern was for the Gadarene way of life; His first concern was for *people,* particularly sick people. To accept Him into the fabric of their community life and into their hearts would mean that they would have to change their priorities, and they couldn't do *that!* Luke says that they were "taken with great fear" (8:37), and so—"Get out." GADARA—LOVE IT OR LEAVE IT!

Jesus got out of Gadara, and He never came back. It was their first and last encounter with the Lord of life, and they blew it.

In some ways the American way of life, as we know it, approximates the way of life in Gadara. The problem among the Gadarenes was that they not only loved their way of life—they worshiped it, and therefore they could not acknowledge and worship and accept the priorities of the Lord of all life.

That is why Pastor Hansen says that a new kind of bumper sticker is in order in our country—one that reads:

AMERICA—LOVE IT BUT DON'T WORSHIP IT

There is a lot of love in America. It is a rich and beautiful land that God has given us, and we love it as the land of the free and the home of the brave. We have not done badly in sharing, through our love, this great bounty with which the Lord has blessed us. But there is also a lot that needs to be changed. That's what America is all about. The people who laid the foundations of our common life built into our system of government a series of checks and balances in order that no one branch should dominate the other. They created a flexibility that leaves open the process of peaceful change. And that suggests another bumper sticker that should read:

AMERICA—CHANGE IT BUT DON'T DESTROY IT

Each of us has his own ideas about how the life of the nation should be changed. Businessmen have one idea, labor another, policemen another, black leaders another, educators, Republicans, Democrats have theirs. But the priorities that are called for today are priorities that must be measured by the stature of Jesus Christ. The American way must be modeled on His way—a way that insists upon truth, upon a mercy and justice that reach out from the success centers to the tombs, out to respond to the deepest of human needs, out to those who have been left out of the good way of life.

The much-discussed conversion of Charles Colson reflects our loss of respect for religious impact. Much of the press and many in governmental circles view his conversion with extreme scepticism and disdain. In an editorial, William Buckley (who is not exactly an evangelical Christian) says, "To say that you have discovered Christ in this secular society of ours, is to say something that causes people to wince with embarrassment. Christ is something to be discovered only between the hours of ten and noon on Sunday . . . by Billy Graham or by a bearded young man on the corner of Hollywood and Vine."

Let it cause embarrassment, if it will, to those who are too sophisticated to believe that the God of Israel and the God of history and the God of our Lord Jesus Christ is the Lord of all the earth and of all the nations—and that He is personally Lord of you and me. I have met Christ, Have you?

Malcom Muggeridge, the salty commentator of Great Britain, says this, "I see it is as one of the greatest ironies of our ironical time that the Christian message should be withdrawn from consideration just when it is needed most desperately to save man's reason if not his soul. It is as though the Salvation Army band, valiantly and patiently waiting through the long years for the Judgment Day, should, when it comes at last . . . throw away their instruments and flee in terror . . . ."

In a sense *every day* is Judgment Day, and in a sense,

every day is the day of salvation; and the salvation of the
nation rests, as it does with every man, woman, and child,
on the empty cross of Jesus Christ—upon His righteousness and justice. He Himself is the generating power who
gives life to a nation and to the world.

We *must* make the change in America.

We might make one last inclusive bumper sticker for
our cars and our hearts:

AMERICA—LOVE IT AND CHANGE IT

I wouldn't attempt to "gild the lily" here by adding a
sermon of my own to this stirring one of Bill Hansen's. I
want only to say that I believe the time has come when
*every one of us* should look into his own life and say:

> Search me, O God, and know my heart: try me
> and know my thoughts: And see if there be
> any wicked way in me, and lead me in the way
> everlasting.
>                                   Psalms 139:23, 24

*Then* we shall prove the truth of the Latin words on the
Great Seal: GOD HAS FAVORED OUR UNDERTAKING. *Our*
God and *our* country; separate them and the worst of our
miserable fears can come true.

Now "our" country—when you come right down to
it—means "my" country and your country, and to keep it
free we have to keep ourselves free from the fears that

would destroy all of us. To be fit to live in a free society we must be free *individually*—and we are a long, long way from that right now. There isn't a man or woman alive in this world who isn't afraid of something or someone; far from being free from fear in our individual lives, the truth is that fear snaps at our heels all through life—like a sheriff's bloodhound snapping at the heels of a guilty criminal. Fear is a universal affliction; some say it is a universal instinct.

Some years ago Basil King wrote a book called *The Conquest of Fear*. He preached it with these words:

> When I say that during most of my conscious life I have been a prey to fears I take it for granted that I am expressing the case of the majority of people. I cannot remember the time when a dread of one kind or another was not in the air. In childhood it was the fear of going to bed . . . . Later it was the fear of school . . . . Later still there was the experience . . . of waking in the morning with a feeling of dismay at what we have to do on getting up . . . . Fear dogs one of us in one way and another in another, but everyone in some way . . . The mother is afraid for her children. The father is afraid for his business. The clerk is afraid for his job . . . . There is hardly a man who is not afraid that some other man will do him a bad turn. There is

hardly a woman who is not afraid that things
she craves may be denied her, or that what she
loves may be snatched away . . . . I am ready
to guess that all the miseries wrought by sin
and sickness put together would not equal
those we bring on ourselves by the means
which perhaps we do least to counteract. . . .

*Phobia* is another word for fear—and we are up to
our necks in phobias. Dr. J. Wallace Hamilton lists some
of them in *Ride the Wild Horses:*

Their name is legion, and they are all bad.
There is acrophobia, or fear of height; claus-
trophobia, the fear of closed places;
agoraphobia, the fear of open places;
neophobia, fear of the new; pathophobia, fear
of disease; photophobia, fear of lights; sperm-
ophobia, fear of germs; ergophobia, fear of
work; (that one isn't in the dictionary yet, but it
is so prevalent that it *will* be soon—perhaps in
the next edition). More than seventy-five
phobias are listed, all the way from
ereuthophobia, fear of blushing (we could do
with a little more of that one!) to phobophobia,
fear of all things.

These are abnormal, irrational fears, not
funny but tragic. Monstrous evil comes out of
misused fear, fear that overshoots its mark,
and they all illustrate and underscore what we

are trying to say—that our basic problem is not
to get rid of fear, but how to use it as God meant
it to be used—as the beginning, as the starting
point of wisdom.

There is wisdom in that statement. There is also wisdom in Dr. Hamilton's contention that *all* fear is not bad,
and that *some* fears are actually good and wholesome and
necessary to the good life of a man and a nation. We
should, for instance, have a good strong fear of rattle-
snakes, of drunks driving high-speed cars on our highways, or children eating toadstools mistaken for mush-
rooms.

There are two kinds of fear: dirty fears and clean fears.
Or, as Dr. Richard R. Marrett puts it, "There are fears
that paralyze and fears that instruct. There are fears that
cleanse and make us healthy, and fears that make us
neurotics." There are fears that stimulate knowledge (it
was our fear of polio that gave us Dr. Salk; it was our fear
of ignorance that gave us our colleges and public schools;
it was fear of pain that gave us hospitals). The tough
whaling captain in *Moby Dick* says, "I will have no man on
my ship who is not afraid of a whale."

General Patton had a great reputation of being fearless
and bold. But the general borrowed a saying from Benjamin Franklin and admitted that he was often afraid.
Ben said, "I never take counsel of my fears." He hit the
bull's-eye on the target with that. What everyone of us
has to do, if we are to be free in a free America, is to
decide whether we are going to listen to our dirty fears or

to our cleansing Christ and God. When our trust is in Him, we *really* conquer fear. Like the disciples of Jesus, we are all afloat on a stormy sea, in this age of fear and terror; like them, we must learn that He is still Master of all seas, all storms.

When the Russians swept into Germany and set up their garrisons over the people of that sad land, there was a mayor in a little town who, like all the people there, must have been afraid of what would happen. But he took counsel of his Christ, and walked into the Russian headquarters and said to the commandant, "We will obey every command of yours that is not in conflict with the teachings of our religion, but do not ask us to do anything contrary to the commands of Christ. That we will not do. You may starve us, imprison us, threaten to shoot us, but we will not do it. We will die first."

That was the counsel of God, an assertion that to be afraid of man is a denial of Christ, a conviction that our own protection against fear individually or nationally or internationally, is *faith*. That is Truth Number 1, in the history of every man and nation on the face of the earth.

# 9

# Not in Washington, But in Your Heart

So the lust for freedom is in the air we breathe, in this country of ours. It's something in the blood, in the heart. But there are storm signals all over the place, warning us that as a famous free democracy we're headed for the grave—with one foot on a banana peel.

This past year, every time I have switched on our radio or TV, I have seen and heard an endless story of more and more corruption, from the national to the local level, and one grows sick at heart over it all. Like a huge boil that has been growing beneath the surface, it is erupting from Maine to Florida. It's easy to become weary of the whole miserable business, and a temptation to turn the switch to a comedy program, just for relief. It is also very tempting to just cop out and sit it out and do nothing about it but shake our heads in disbelief.

But whenever that feeling comes over me, I think of the innocent trusting faces of my grandchildren and something inside me shouts, "What about *their* rights, *their* future?" I hear the politicians shouting about the next election; I'm more concerned with the next generation. These children and grandchildren, too, listen to the wild-eyed, stupid pessimists who suggest that we all turn tail and run and give up because "What's the use? I'm just one person; what can I do about it?" Or they see the dead being carried out of a building that has been bombed by cowards who put their faith in violence as a weapon to destroy a so-called oppressive government! It isn't a very pretty picture.

Just recently I read this comment, about such goings-on:

> The daily spectacle of atrocious acts has sti-
> fled all feeling of pity in the hearts of men.
> When every hour we see or hear of an act of

dreadful cruelty we lose all feeling of humanity. Crime no longer horrifies us. We smile at the enormities of youth. We condone passion, when we should understand that the unrestrained emotions of man produce chaos. Once we were a nation of self-control and austerity and had a reverence for life and justice. This is true no longer. We prefer our politicians, particularly if they swagger with youth and are accomplished jesters and liars. We love entertainment, even in law, even in government. Unless we reform, our terrible fate is inevitable.

No, this was not written about us by some modern columnist or critic; these are the closing words of a lawyer named Marcus Tullius Cicero (106–43 B.C.), at the trial of one Sextus Roscius. (I read it in Taylor Caldwell's book, *Pillar of Iron;* if you haven't read it, get it today!) Cicero—and the Rome that ruled the world!! *Sic transit Roma. Sic transit America.*

We have always had this problem, in every corner of the earth: *The problem of the loss of a personal sense of responsibility, the problem of passing the buck to the emperor, or the senate, or the president—to anyone but ourselves.* Corruption is nothing new; it is as old as the apple tree in Eden.

When Gerald Ford took office as president of The United States, he said that the morality and integrity of the government is as good or as bad as the morality and integrity of the individual voter casting his ballot in the voting booth. Sure, we had Watergate—and a lot of us tried to laugh it off with, "Oh, it's nothing new. Besides, *I* didn't do it." Didn't you? Were we not all partially guilty for it all—by lowering our personal standards? Publicist Ed Lipscomb has written: "Freedom rests, and always will, on individual responsibility, individual integrity, individual effort, individual courage, and individual religious faith. It does not rest in Washington. It rests with you and me." Right! The destiny of this country isn't lodged in the White House, or in the halls of Congress, but *right in your own living room.*

I say we have all sinned here, and come short of the glory of God; the sinners are not confined to a president and a few aides; we are *all* guilty. Our public officials are people like you and me. They were raised in homes like yours and mine. They had the same training or the same lack of it, in their homes, schools, churches, or synagogues. *We* stand guilty of relaxing our constant vigilance for freedom. That's one rule about freedom that we too often overlook. It isn't a gift of the saints established and made secure in us forever and ever, but rather a quality of character which we must develop and protect for ourselves. The price of freedom is *constant* vigilance. Let it die in the individual American heart, and no Constitution, no law, no court can save it.

Sit down now and read the Seventy-eighth Psalm, and find out what happens when the vigilance is relaxed, when a people get careless, when the shout to let freedom ring dies down to a whisper. If God, in the psalm, did not spare His own, He certainly will not spare us until we return to Him like the prodigals we are.

Just after last Christmas, there was a news item in the *New York Times* about a policewoman (*not* in uniform!) who drove around the streets of her city in a car loaded with new portable TV sets. She didn't say that she was selling them for any TV firm or store; she told her prospective customers that her boyfriend had stolen them. She sold every one of them. Some of the purchasers took them home, some bought them and sold them again, some asked if she could get some more. Only one person turned her down!

See what I mean? Our freedom isn't so much a national accomplishment or virtue as it is a *personal* quality. Freedom is self-discipline, the privilege or right to choose the right from the wrong. When we condone that which is wrong—when we play games with the truth—our patriotism is a mockery, and we are traitors to the freedom we announce to the world.

Susan Coolidge put it well:

He serves his country best
Who lives pure life and doeth righteous deeds,
And walks straight paths, however others stray,
And leaves his sons an uttermost bequest,
A stainless record which all men may read.

This is the better way. Yes, we've had Watergate, yes, we've had corruption—not just in our time, but from the time of the first politician, in every age and hour. There have always been a few rotten apples in the barrel—but we get rid of them, and we have no right to put down all the people because of a few bad ones—no right to throw away all the good apples in the barrel because there are a few rotten ones. But I think we should have an *E* for *Effort,* at least. We do try. We do correct the government when it errs. We do fight the mistakes of our legislators when they pass a bad law—and more often than not they repeal the law. But *we* have to protest. We have to make the effort, each on his own. And while we're about it, let's clean up our own back yards, as individuals—that is, the poorer parts of our lives which we try to hide—the bad thoughts, the little sneaky things we do when no one is looking or hearing. There's an old saying, "You take care of the pennies and the dollars will take care of themselves." Well, if we watch the little things in our lives to see that they are right, then we will be able to handle the big things in the right way.

If we are ever to see any real, honest-to-goodness improvement in our national morality, it must begin on a one-to-one basis. We simply have to face ourselves, take a long, hard look at our personal lives—and start to "put our money where our mouth is." In other words, we have to be scrupulously honest, caring about our neighbor's rights, *right now,* right where we stand this minute. True, it will cost us, for righteousness, while it "exalteth a nation," always costs—*but it has never lost a nation.* It may seem that unrighteousness is winning for a time, but let us remember the story of the turtle and the hare. The race does not always go to the swift, fast-buck, money-

under-the-table crowd. In the end, they lose. God or-
dained it that way.

To put it in a nutshell, I'm fed up with the pessimists
who are so busy making preparations for this country's
funeral. There have been a lot of such preparers, in times
past, when this country faced desperate problems—but
we always came through it, and found ourselves stronger
than ever. I'm disgusted with those who are trying to shift
the basis of our national life from God to greedy prosperity and to merely human opinions and operations. The
American people have a reputation for rolling up their
sleeves when trouble comes, and for facing it together;
they have done it often, and they will do it again. I have
faith in my God—and in my country. And I have no
sympathy or patience whatever with the senator who
declared on television that "The old-time religion is in-
adequate to meet today's complex problems. It sounds
very beautiful and simple, but it will not suffice to meet
today's need . . ." (or words to that effect). I suggest
that the senator try practicing that old-time religion,
before he condemns it—and do a little reading in the
history of other nations that have said much the same
thing—and have perished for it.

Thank heaven, he is not typical of all senators
—particularly of our younger senators. There are
healthy, wonderful signs of hope in these younger ones
in their quest for reality, honesty, true goals for their
lives, genuine interest in reverence to God, and respect
for this God-given country. More and more young men
are aiming at public office; they are demanding good

government. They are willing to get their feet wet in this political storm that sweeps the nation—and to preserve the truly good, sound institutions, and to honestly examine past mistakes in an unbiased manner. They seem willing to correct them, even if it takes a hard, uphill struggle against some who, in their ease and complacency, do not want to "rock the boat." Let the seasoned ones who have been on the road a long time communicate with these young hopefuls, and work with them —and above all pray that God will inspire and strengthen them for the incredibly arduous task of unraveling the knots in our national life.

And let *us* support *them!* How? I think there are two ways in which we can support them, and fight for a better and better America.

One way is strictly practical; it has to do with something we can *do*. We can stop this nonsense of going around like gloomy killjoys singing the blues about the awful shape we're in and what a rotten lot we are. We've been in bad shape before; we have had to face greater threats to our national security than we face now, and I for one don't intend to throw in the sponge before the fight is half over. We can walk with our heads up, our eyes to the future and not on the past, and in the faith that God who has never let us down, will not let us down now.

We can accept the fact of change—whether we like to change or not. The world of today isn't the world in which we over thirty grew up, by a long shot, and we'd better admit it and adjust to it, if we want to get along and not go down. The situations in every nation change *every day*. Doctors don't shut up tuberculosis patients in rooms with closed and sealed windows; they have learned that the thing to do is to open those windows and let in the fresh air. We should learn something from that—learn enough to keep our minds and our hearts open to whatever light we can find; learn enough to accept any new light that will help us, any change that will contribute some good to our growth. I'm not talking about change for the sake of change, of revolution for revolution's sake, of being a "rebel" just because it's fun to be a rebel; that's stupid. This country was born in rebellion against tyranny; that's the kind of rebellion I like—and the kind of change I like.

We can support them by refusing to get all snarled up with those who preach disunity among our people—disunity among whites and blacks, rich and poor, Protestants and Catholics and Jews, management and labor, or whatever. We are all *one*—and we should act as one. There is no room here for rabble-rousers, witch-hunters, racists, bigots, or bullies. We have fought too hard and too long for this equality we have in America—for this freedom—to lose it now in strife between ourselves.

A friend in California knows a man who came here from Greece; he worked fifty years to establish himself on his farm. That farm is a beauty spot for all who see it, and that Greek-American is beautiful when he says, "No one can run down this wonderful country to us. We love it, and we will fight for it!" That family came here with little worldly goods, but with a great faith in the American Dream, and that Dream became a reality in them.

They love this country more than some of the "natives" I have known. Old Artemus Ward, famous wit of another generation, said in his humorous way, "Too much good blud was spilt in courtin' and marryin' that highly respectable female, the 'Goddess of Liberty,' to git a divorce from her now." So say I.

We can go to the voting booth like intelligent and informed human beings, and vote according to our consciences and not at the command of windy politicians whom we suspect.

We can stop talking and go to work on problems local and national. We can begin where we are, and get involved where we are. That's a privilege that is denied in a large part of this world.

We can get interested in our schools, where the foundations of freedom are laid in our youth. We can know what they are being taught—and maybe some things that they should not be taught.

We can do something about what we call *welfare*—the feeding and care of the poor, the Christian spirit of love put into action. We can do a lot more than we are doing now in this department; we can also crack down with a firm *no*, on those who could support themselves if they wanted to, but who use welfare as a racket.

We can get off the sidelines and in the game. We can prove our gratitude to our founding fathers in *action* more than in words. All this reminds me of the story about the liberated slave who came to tell President Lincoln that he could not accept his freedom as a free gift. He handed the president a silver dollar. The president looked at the dollar and at the grateful little man, then took his arm and led him over to a window from which they could see a big field filled with the graves of dead soldiers. He asked the man gently if he thought one silver dollar could buy back all those lost lives that had been sacrificed for his freedom. There were tears in the eyes of both of them as Lincoln told the former slave that there was only one way in which he could 'pay' for his freedom: It was to walk in love and gratitude, and to *live* as a free man. That has meaning for *all* of us.

This is what we can all do—personally. But we'll need help and inspiration to do it—help from God, the Author and Giver of our freedom. I think we can get that inspiration from His Word—specifically from Galatians 5:13–25. Let me suggest that you may get it by reading and digesting the wonderful words as we find them in the edition known as Today's English Version, *Good News for Modern Man,* published by the American Bible Society:

> As for you, my brothers, you were called to be free. But do not let this freedom become an excuse for letting your physical desires rule you. Instead, let love make you serve one another. For the whole Law is summed up in one commandment: "Love your neighbor as yourself." But if you act like animals, hurting and harming each other, then watch out, or you will completely destroy one another.
>
> This is what I say: let the Spirit direct your lives, and do not satisfy the desires of the

human nature. For what our human nature wants is opposed to what the Spirit wants, and what the Spirit wants is opposed to what human nature wants: the two are enemies, and this means that you cannot do what you want to do. If the Spirit leads you, then you are not subject to the Law.

What human nature does is quite plain. It shows itself in immoral, filthy, and indecent actions . . . People become enemies, they fight, become jealous, angry, and ambitious. They separate into parties and groups . . . I warn you now as I have before: those who do these things will not receive the Kingdom of God.

But the Spirit produces love, joy, peace, patience, kindness, goodness, faithfulness, humility, and self-control. There is no law against such things as these. And those who belong to Christ Jesus have put to death their human nature, with all its passions and desires. The Spirit has given us life; he must also control our lives.

If there is a better prescription for producing Christian citizens in a Christian America, I haven't seen it yet.

# Addenda

Highbrow and scholarly writers (I'm not one of them!) often add, at the end of their books, a thing they call *Addenda*. Now Addenda sometimes is something they wanted to get into their books, but often couldn't find a place for, so they added it at the end. There are just a few things I think should be added to what I have said in these pages, and here they are.

The first is a prayer—the first prayer ever offered in
the Congress of the United States. It was offered in
December of 1777 by the Reverend J. Duche at a moment when things looked bad for the people of this
nation. It went like this:

> O Lord, our Heavenly Father, High and
> mighty King of kings, our Lord of lords, who
> dost from Thy throne behold all the dwellers
> on earth and reignest with power supreme and
> uncontrolled over all the Kingdoms, look down
> in mercy, we beseech Thee, on these American
> States, who have fled to Thee from the rod of
> the oppressor, and thrown themselves on Thy
> gracious protection, desiring henceforth to be
> dependent only on Thee; to Thee, they have
> appealed for the righteousness of their cause;
> to Thee do they now look up for that counte-
> nance and support which Thou alone canst
> give; take them therefore, Heavenly Father,
> under Thy nurturing care; give them wisdom
> in Council and valor in the field; defeat the
> malicious designs of our cruel adversaries;
> convince them of the unrighteousness of
> their cause; and if they persist in their san-
> guinary purpose. O let the voice of Thine own
> unerring justice, sounding in their hearts, con-
> strain them to drop the weapons of war from
> their unnerved hands in the day of battle!

Be thou present, O God of wisdom, and direct the councils of this honorable assembly; enable them to settle things on the best and surest foundation. That the scene of blood may be speedily closed; that order, harmony and peace may be effectually restored, and truth and justice, religion and piety prevail and flourish among Thy people. Preserve the health of their bodies and the vigor of their minds; shower down on them, and on the millions they here represent, such temporal blessings as Thou seest expedient for them in this world, and crown them with everlasting glory in the world to come. All this we ask in the name and through the merits of Jesus Christ, The Son, our Saviour. AMEN

Perfect, for Congress—*and* for a nation being born! That was prayer—which is in the American blood. There is another divine quality in that blood: music. Long ago, Walt Whitman wrote a little poem that began with the line, "I hear America singing, the varied carols I hear." Some of the great American songs we sing are close to being carols, or songs of joy, or even hymns. Take, for instance, Katherine Lee Bates's "America the Beautiful." Augustine Smith, who was at one time the most prominent American authority on music in religion, said that this song should be in every hymnal "because it recognizes so clearly and emphasizes so fully the fact that

America alone and unaided cannot make its dream come
true. It is only God who can "shed His grace" and 'crown
good with brotherhood.'" That "shed His grace" should
move us deeply. And there are other lines here that really
grip and hold the patriotic heart.

Can any of us sing "O beautiful for spacious skies"
without a faster heartbeat? Have you ever watched the
sunset beyond the Rockies? Have you ever seen a sunrise
over the Capitol in Washington? If you can be unmoved
at such a sight, you're half dead. Spacious skies! The
great wide spaceless dome of beautiful blue that lifts our
eyes and hearts upward—the sky over America. I sometimes think it is even more beautiful than the good earth
beneath it; the two together complement each other, and
their morning stars sing together. Even our streaming jet
planes with their trails of smoke cannot detract from its
beauty. I have flown many times at 30,000 feet and
higher and believe me, the sky up there is as glorious as it
is on the ground. Beautiful—*beautiful,* as only the hand-
work of God can be.

"For amber waves of grain . . . ." Have you seen a
Kansas wheat field bowing in the wind, rolling like the
waves of an endless inland sea? God gave us the land;
God gave us the seed; God sent the rain; God led us to the
point where we have become breadbasket to the world.
Maybe there are times (in drought, for instance) when it
doesn't look so good, especially to the wheat farmer
—times when the crop is thin—but somewhere along the
line, even then, the old system of checks and balances

gets to work and the next yield is better. As a child, I can remember plentiful years of cotton crops in the South, when everything was just right, when sun and rain were balanced—and I can remember some very lean years in which the boll weevil got his way. I can also remember the thrill of standing with my father in the midst of a thick stand of maize in North Texas, feeling within myself the first stirrings of love for this rich, fertile, and beautiful land.

"For purple mountain majesties, Above the fruited plain . . . ." God put great mountains in our land, I often think, to keep us humble. Whenever you come to the place where you think you are *somebody*, someone big, go out and look at a mountain—a mountain so high that its purple top seems to scrape the floor of heaven. It rings old bells in our hearts when we read in Numbers 27:12 that God said to Moses, "Get thee up into this mount . . . and see the land which I have given . . . ." Try it some time. Go up there and see, as far as your eye will reach, the land He has given you. When a tourist asked an old Swiss mountain climber why he wanted to climb *any* mountain, the old fellow said, "Because up there you are high above everything; you are on your own; you are up there all alone with God." Thank God for the mountains He gives us to climb, both figuratively and physically.

Down from the mountains plunge the rivers which bring life to "fruited" plains so necessary to our existence. George Herbert said, "A mountain and a river are good neighbours." We not only love them for their natural beauty; we need them to survive. Get rid of our mountains and you lose the glory of the dusky evening purple and the rocky fortresses guarding our rolling plains. We should know that—without being told—but we don't act as though we knew it. In the name of progress we have dug great tunnels through mountains to get somewhere faster; today we are drilling into the Rockies for oil. We need oil, but I for one hate to see the mountains of America torn apart or covered with oil derricks. I know people must have houses to live in, but I resent the sight of lovely plains and haunting deserts covered with rows upon row of cheap, ugly houses that look as though they would be gone with the first wind that hits them.

We have polluted our rivers beyond belief, and we have been anything but good stewards of the Creator in destroying the beauty and the bounty He has put in our hands. Forgive us, Father, for we *know* what we have done!

But of course it is that line about the grace of God and the brotherhood of man, in Katherine Bates's song, that really gets to us. God *has* shed His grace on *us;* He *has* given us wealth and power that is overwhelming—and He intended us to use all that—not for the profit of a privileged few—not to make us overproud and boastful and even obnoxious to those nations which have less. He intended us to use it all to help build a brotherhood of mankind, from sea to shining sea.

We just haven't done that. We have become too sleek,

too fat, too lazy, too greedy; we have forgotten our
source of grace and how to draw on Him through dili-
gent practice of His Way and Will among ourselves and
among other peoples. It is no small wonder that foreigners resent the way some Americans flaunt their
wealth when they travel abroad.

Saint Paul, who was a great traveler, said that he had
become "all things to all men." What did he mean by that?
The Living Bible explains it in 1 Corinthians 9:22, 23:

> . . . I don't act as though I know it all and
> don't say they are foolish; the result is that
> they are willing to let me help them. Yes, what-
> ever a person is like, I try to find common
> ground with him so that he will let me tell him
> about Christ and let Christ save him. I do this to
> get the Gospel to them . . . .

That's what we should be doing. Paul was a missionary,
and he had his priorities right. He went among the
foreign Gentiles; he ate their food; he was gracious in
accepting their hospitality, just as it was, without wailing
loudly that it wasn't the style of living to which he was
accustomed. He set the mold for the missionaries who
came after him.

In a sense, we Americans should all be missionaries to
our own people—as well as to those in other lands—if we
really believe that the grace of God is available to all the
people in all the world. They too, in a global brotherhood

of man, may come to live together more abundantly under the grace of a universal Father who alone can give us peace, liberty, and happiness.

I began this little book with a song I had written to sing in our "God and Country" appearances all across the country. Let me end it with another we have used for the same purpose.

Almighty God of my Fathers,
Give me the courage to stand
And speak the truth I know, to friend and foe,
And to walk with my brothers, hand in hand.
Help me to see clearly, Father,
What you would have me do,
Give me the strength for the task,
That's all I ask—to honor the Red, White and Blue.
Restore a right spirit within my heart,
To want for every man, liberty,
And when I see oppression, help me do my part
To right the wrong, and bring harmony.
Almighty God of my Fathers,
Humbly I come; hear my plea—
Give us the grace to see
Truth and Liberty go hand in hand
In a land that is free!

# IN CONGRESS, JULY 4, 1776.

# A DECLARATION

## By THE REPRESENTATIVES OF THE UNITED STATES OF AMERICA, IN GENERAL CONGRESS ASSEMBLED.

*When in the Course of human Events,* it becomes necessary for one People to dissolve the Political Bands which have connected them with another, and to assume among the Powers of the Earth, the separate and equal Station to which the Laws of Nature and of Nature's God entitle them, a decent Respect to the Opinions of Mankind requires that they should declare the causes which impel them to the Separation.

We hold these Truths to be self-evident, that all Men are created equal, that they are endowed by their Creator with certain unalienable Rights, that among these are Life, Liberty, and the Pursuit of Happiness—That to secure these Rights, Governments are instituted among Men, deriving their just Powers from the Consent of the Governed, that whenever any Form of Government becomes destructive of these Ends, it is the Right of the People to alter or to abolish it, and to institute new

Government, laying its Foundation on such Principles, and organizing its Powers in such Form, as to them shall seem most likely to effect their Safety and Happiness. Prudence, indeed, will dictate that Governments long established should not be changed for light and transient Causes; and accordingly all Experience hath shewn, that Mankind are more disposed to suffer, while Evils are sufferable, than to right themselves by abolishing the Forms to which they are accustomed. But when a long Train of Abuses and Usurpations, pursuing invariably the same Object, evinces a Design to reduce them under absolute Despotism, it is their Right, it is their Duty, to throw off such Government, and to provide new Guards for their future Security. Such has been the patient Sufferance of these Colonies; and such is now the Necessity which constrains them to alter their former Systems of Government. The History of the present King of Great-Britain is a History of repeated Injuries and Usurpations, all having in direct Object the Establishment of an absolute Tyranny over these States. To prove this, let Facts be submitted to a candid World.

He has refused his Assent to Laws, the most wholesome and necessary for the public Good.

He has forbidden his Governors to pass Laws of immediate and pressing Importance, unless suspended in their Operation till his Assent should be obtained; and when so suspended he has utterly neglected to attend to them.

He has refused to pass other Laws for the Accommodation of large Districts of People, unless those People would relinquish the Right of Representation in the Legislature, a Right inestimable to them, and formidable to Tyrants only.

He has called together Legislative Bodies at Places unusual, uncomfortable, and distant from the Depository of their public Records, for the sole Purpose of fatiguing them into Compliance with his Measures.

He has dissolved Representative Houses repeatedly, for opposing with manly Firmness his Invasions on the Rights of the People.

He has refused for a long Time, after such dissolutions, to cause others to be elected; whereby the Legislative Powers, incapable of Annihilation, have returned to the People at large for their exercise; the State remaining in the mean time exposed to all the Dangers of Invasion from without, and Convulsions within.

He has endeavoured to prevent the Population of these States; for that Purpose obstructing the Laws for Naturalization of Foreigners; refusing to pass others to encourage their Migrations hither, and raising the Conditions of new Appropriations of Lands.

He has obstructed the Administration of Justice, by refusing his Assent to Laws for establishing Judiciary Powers.

He has made Judges dependent on his Will alone, for the Tenure of their Offices, and the Amount and Payment of their Salaries.

He has erected a Multitude of new Offices, and sent hither Swarms of Officers to harass our People, and eat out their Substance.

He has kept among us, in Times of Peace, Standing Armies, without the consent of our Legislatures.

He has affected to render the Military independent of and superior to the Civil Power.

He has combined with others to subject us to a Jurisdiction foreign to our Constitution, and unacknowledged by our Laws; giving his Assent to their Acts of pretended Legislation:

For quartering large Bodies of Armed Troops among us:

For protecting them, by a mock Trial, from Punishment for any Murders which they should commit on the Inhabitants of these States:

For cutting off our Trade with all Parts of the World:

For imposing Taxes on us without our Consent:

For depriving us, in many Cases, of the Benefits of Trial by Jury:

For transporting us beyond Seas to be tried for pretended Offences:

For abolishing the free System of English Laws in a neighbouring Province, establishing therein an arbitrary Government, and enlarging its Boundaries, so as to render it at once an Example and fit Instrument for introducing the same absolute Rule into these Colonies:

For taking away our Charters, abolishing our most valuable Laws, and altering fundamentally the Forms of our Governments:

For suspending our own Legislatures, and declaring themselves invested with Power to legislate for us in all Cases whatsoever.

He has abdicated Government here, by declaring us out of his Protection and waging War against us.

He has plundered our Seas, ravaged our Coasts, burnt our Towns, and destroyed the Lives of our People.

He is, at this Time, transporting large Armies of foreign Mercenaries to compleat the Works of Death, Desolation, and Tyranny, already begun with circumstances of Cruelty and Perfidy, scarcely paralleled in the most barbarous Ages, and totally unworthy the Head of a civilized Nation.

He has constrained our fellow Citizens taken Captive on the high Seas to bear Arms against their Country, to become the Executioners of their Friends and Brethren, or to fall themselves by their Hands.

He has excited domestic Insurrections amongst us, and has endeavoured to bring on the Inhabitants of our Frontiers, the merciless Indian Savages, whose known Rule of Warfare, is an undistinguished Destruction, of all Ages, Sexes and Conditions.

In every stage of these Oppressions we have Petitioned for Redress in the most humble Terms: Our repeated Petitions have been answered only by repeated Injury. A Prince, whose Character is thus marked by every act which may define a Tyrant, is unfit to be the Ruler of a free People.

Nor have we been wanting in Attentions to our British Brethren. We have warned them from Time to Time of attempts by their Legislature to extend an unwarrantable Jurisdiction over us. We have reminded them of the Circumstances of our Emigration and Settlement here. We have appealed to their native Justice and Magnanimity, and we have conjured them by the Ties of our common Kindred to disavow these Usurpations, which, would inevitably interrupt our Connections and Correspondence. They too have been deaf to the Voice of Justice and of Consanguinity. We must, therefore, acquiesce in the Necessity, which denounces our Separation, and hold them, as we hold the rest of Mankind, Enemies in War, in Peace, Friends.

We, therefore, the Representatives of the UNITED STATES OF AMERICA, in GENERAL CONGRESS, Assembled, appealing to the Supreme Judge of the World for the Rectitude of our Intentions, do, in the Name, and by Authority of the good People of these Colonies, solemnly Publish and Declare, That these United Colonies are, and of Right ought to be, FREE AND INDEPENDENT STATES; that they are absolved from all Allegiance to the British Crown, and that all political Connection between them and the State of Great-Britain, is and ought to be totally dissolved; and that as FREE AND INDEPENDENT STATES, they have full Power to levy War, conclude Peace, contract Alliances, establish Commerce, and to do all other Acts and Things which INDEPENDENT STATES may of right do. And for the support of this Declaration, with a firm Reliance on the Protection of divine Providence, we mutually pledge to each other our Lives, our Fortunes, and our sacred Honor.

*Signed by* ORDER *and in* BEHALF *of the* CONGRESS, JOHN HANCOCK, PRESIDENT.

### NEW-HAMPSHIRE.

*Josiah Bartlett,*
*W^m· Whipple,*
*Matthew Thornton.*

### MASSACHUSETTS-BAY.

*Sam^l· Adams,*
*John Adams,*
*Rob^t· Treat Paine,*
*Elbridge Gerry.*

### RHODE-ISLAND AND PROVIDENCE, &c.

*Step. Hopkins,*
*William Ellery.*

### CONNECTICUT.

*Roger Sherman,*
*Sam^l· Huntington,*
*W^m· Williams,*
*Oliver Wolcott.*

### DELAWARE.

*Cæsar Rodney,*
*Geo. Read,*
*Tho. M:Kean.*

### MARYLAND.

*Samuel Chase,*
*W^m· Paca,*
*Tho^s· Stone,*
*Charles Carroll, of Carroll-*
*ton.*

### VIRGINIA.

*George Wythe,*
*Richard Henry Lee,*
*Th^s· Jefferson,*
*Benj^a· Harrison,*
*Tho^s· Nelson, j^r·*

### NEW-YORK.

*W^m· Floyd,*
*Phil. Livingston,*
*Fran^s· Lewis,*
*Lewis Morris.*

### NEW-JERSEY.

*Rich^d· Stockton,*
*Jno. Witherspoon,*
*Fra^s· Hopkinson,*
*John Hart,*
*Abra. Clark.*

### PENNSYLVANIA.

*Rob^t· Morris,*
*Benjamin Rush,*
*Benja. Franklin,*
*John Morton,*
*Geo. Clymer,*
*Ja^s· Smith,*
*Geo. Taylor,*
*James Wilson,*
*Geo. Ross.*
*Francis Lightfoot Lee,*
*Carter Braxton.*

### NORTH-CAROLINA.

*W^m· Hooper,*
*Joseph Hewes,*
*John Penn.*

### SOUTH-CAROLINA.

*Edward Rutledge,*
*Tho^s· Heyward, jun^r·*
*Thomas Lynch, jun^r·*
*Arthur Middleton.*

### GEORGIA.

*Button Gwinnett,*
*Lyman Hall,*
*Geo. Walton.*